All That We Can Be

All That We Can Be

Black Leadership
and Racial Integration
the Army Way

CHARLES C. MOSKOS

AND

JOHN SIBLEY BUTLER

A Twentieth Century Fund Book

BasicBooks
A Division of HarperCollins*Publishers*

The Twentieth Century Fund sponsors and supervises timely analyses of economic policy, foreign affairs, and domestic political issues. Not-for-profit and nonpartisan, the Fund was founded in 1919 and endowed by Edward A. Filene.

Copyright © 1996 by The Twentieth Century Fund, Inc.

Published by BasicBooks,
A Division of HarperCollins Publishers, Inc.

Designed by Elliott Beard

Library of Congress Cataloging-in-Publication Data
Moskos, Charles C.
    All that we can be : Black leadership and racial integration the
Army way / by Charles C. Moskos and John Sibley Butler.
        p.   cm.
    "A Twentieth Century Fund book."
    Includes index.
    ISBN 0-465-00108-4 (cloth)
    ISBN 0-465-00113-0 (paper)
    1. United States. Army—Afro-Americans.   2. Sociology, Military—
United States.   3. United States—Race relations.   I. Butler, John S.
II. Title.
UB418.A47M67   1996
355'.0089'96073—dc20   96-16570

97 98 99 00 01 ❖/RRD 10 9 8 7 6 5 4 3 2 1

Dedicated to Our Parents

Charles Moskos, Sr. (1900–1979)
Rita Moskos (1910–1954)
T. J. Butler, Sr. (1908–1992);
Gone to Glory

and to Johnnye Mae Sibley Butler
who is still with us

Contents

List of Tables

Foreword

Race has always been the central domestic question for Americans. At times, when it comes to this issue, we seem to be evolving in ways both remarkable and promising. But, even then, there are potent reminders of all that is ugly and intractable about our history of racial divisions. Reflecting this schizophrenia, public discourse about race brings out the best and the worst in Americans. Perhaps most disappointing is how routinely descriptions of the state of relations between blacks and whites and discussions about how to improve them lack openness, clarity, and substance. The poverty of our conversation is not the result of insufficient research and scholarship. Nor is it a product of the frequently stunted political and programmatic debate among serious citizens and public figures. Ultimately, the nation simply seems at a collective loss for words to explain why, despite our nearly obsessive focus on racial tensions, we continue to have more problems that relate to this than to any other aspect of our society.

It has never been easy to deal with the uniquely American problems of slavery and segregation, and the legacy of persistent poverty they created. In fact, the greatest changes in race relations were not the result of an orderly and peaceful development of a national consensus. Rather, in the first case—freeing the slaves—change was imposed by the bloodiest war in our history. In the second—the end of Jim Crow in the South—real movement came as a result of the decisions of a Supreme Court insulated from democratic politics, decisions that had to be enforced by the armed might of the nation, in the form, again, of federal troops.

Despite the decisive role it played in reshaping racial affairs, the American military, for good reasons, is seldom described as being on the cutting edge of social reform. Like most of their counterparts throughout history, the armed services are relatively conservative organizations, committed to preserving the special aspects of military culture that contribute to success in combat. To be sure, they also are a mirror of the larger society, but their leaders work very hard to shape these institutions so that they reflect some aspects of the nation more sharply than others.

This is a book about one of the military services: the Army. It also is, in a sense, a book about what happened when one major American institution, for a variety of complex and compelling reasons, made a decision to do whatever was necessary to achieve substantially full integration and extensive if not completely equal opportunity. It is a story that can teach us much, for although the Army is a special case, it is, after all, constructed from the culture of the larger nation.

Indeed, this book is but part of a larger story about how a deeply troubled major public organization reformed itself, changed central aspects of its character, and won back the support of the American people.

Looking back at the 1970s, more than twenty years after the Army was officially integrated, it was not obvious that such an accomplishment was likely or even possible. The post–Vietnam era was among the low points in the history of the Army. The military services in general were widely unpopular among the American people. Many of the best and the brightest had left the services. The test scores and educational background of the new recruits to the now all-volunteer army had slumped dramatically. And especially among Army units stationed in Germany, racial strife, already common enough in Southeast Asia, had reached epidemic proportions. Yet, if we flash forward to 1996, we find the U.S. Army transformed. The armed services today are almost certainly the most popular public institutions in the nation. Amid sharp post–Cold War cutbacks, the military retains a core of high-quality leadership; more than 90 percent of enlisted men are high school graduates; a retired Afro-American general is perhaps the most popular public figure in the nation. Moreover, and perhaps most significantly, at a time of stark tensions and continuing separation between the races, not only is the Army a thoroughly integrated institution, its members seem at peace with the idea.

Who brought about these changes and how did they do it? Most important, what can society in general learn from the Army experience?

It was with these questions in mind that the Twentieth Century Fund approached Charles Moskos and John Sibley Butler. They represent the ideal team for this effort, with backgrounds that uniquely qualify them for this mission. Both are noted researchers in this field—they have served in and written extensively about the military, and they have extraordinary access to those in the military, at all levels.

In this book, Moskos and Butler not only look at the Army but also try to show the relevance of the Army's experiences to the continuing issue of race in American society. As they make clear, the Army story is not about overcoming all the institution's racial problems; obviously, it has not. Nor is this story merely a recitation of "techniques" used to accomplish a particular mission. The Army story is so important because of how far it has come in overcoming racial problems; it is also important for what it can teach us about what it takes to get the job done—about the possibilities for success when you take the mission seriously, even as a matter of life and death. These lessons need to be sifted, debated, and subjected to further research, but they must not be ignored. We hope that this book will open up new ways of thinking about affirmative action, remedial education, and ultimately, community. America may not "die" if it fails to make more headway against racial divisions, but perhaps something worse will happen: it will lose its soul.

The Twentieth Century Fund has long had an interest in race and society. In the early 1970s, it supported Adam Yarmolinsky's study of the military, *The Military Establishment: Its Impacts on American Society*, which included an examination of race relations and the military. In the late 1980s, the Fund supported Abigail Thernstrom's *Whose Votes Count? Affirmative Action and Minority Voting Rights* and Richard Halloran's *Serving America*. In the 1990s, at the Fund's request, Gordon MacInnes explored the issues of race, poverty, and politics in *Wrong for All the Right Reasons*, and the Fund is now supporting an examination of affirmative action by Lincoln Caplan, an analysis of black entrepreneurship by Thomas Boston, and a volume of essays on equal opportunity.

On behalf of the Trustees of the Twentieth Century Fund, I thank Charles Moskos and John Sibley Butler for this pioneering work. I also want to thank the Rockefeller and Ford foundations for their support for this project.

Richard C. Leone, President
The Twentieth Century Fund
MARCH 1996

Preface

One of the authors of this book benefited from affirmative action—and it was not the black one. Charles Moskos was admitted to Princeton University in 1952 from Albuquerque High School. His deficiencies in mathematics and less than stellar (but decent) grades were overlooked because Princeton wanted to recruit someone from New Mexico. John Sibley Butler is a 1969 graduate of Louisiana State University. He had planned to attend the family alma mater, Southern University, a historically black institution, but in the final moments of decision, his mother and father asked that he attend LSU to be among a small group of black freshmen to integrate that university at the undergraduate level. Some other background is in order. Moskos is the first in his family to complete secondary school. Butler is the fourth generation of his family to receive a college degree. So much for racial stereotypes.

Our book is the collaborative effort of two former draftees, and the Army experience is one we both look back upon with pride. Each of us entered the Army shortly after receiving our baccalaureates: Moskos served in Germany during the late 1950s, Butler is a decorated veteran of the Vietnam War. Each of us entered graduate school in sociology after leaving the Army. Over the years, Moskos has made military sociology his specialty, starting with field research during the Vietnam War. Butler wrote his doctoral dissertation on institutional racism in the military and has continued to write extensively on race relations in the armed forces as well as the self-help tradition in the black community. In another parallel, the first article each of us published dealt with race relations in the Army.[1]

The material in this book comes from diverse sources and much of the data have never been presented before. We conducted surveys from 1992 to 1995 of active-duty soldiers with questions designed to illuminate race relations in the contemporary Army and to allow comparisons with civilian findings. We rely most, however, on our participant observations with soldiers on American bases and in Europe and, in the case of Moskos, with units deployed to Panama, Somalia, Haiti, and the former Yugoslavia. Butler has also interviewed staff members of historically black colleges and universities, institutions that we hold in special regard. We have also had informal discussions with soldiers of all ranks, active and retired, black and white, some of them our friends for two decades. Their insights continue to enlighten our own understanding of race relations in the Army. These data, quantitative and qualitative alike, inform our judgments throughout the text.

Several readers of the manuscript suggested that we

draw parallels between the experience of blacks in the military and that of women or gays and lesbians. We resist this suggestion as it detracts from our central premise: that race is the prime American dilemma and has unique dynamics. False analogies confuse rather than clarify.[2] Indeed, the key point is that the social relations between blacks and whites differ fundamentally from those between women and men, or between gays and straights, or, for that matter, between immigrant groups and native-born Americans. We are even reluctant to make comparisons between American blacks and other peoples of color. For us, the nature of relations between blacks and whites—or perhaps better, between blacks and nonblacks—is unique to American society. Ask yourself: Who is more likely to be considered white in our society, the offspring of a mixed Anglo-Hispanic or European-Asian union, or the offspring of a mixed white-black marriage?

This brings us to the matter of terminology. We use the terms "black American" and "Afro-American" interchangeably. We prefer Afro-American to African-American for several reasons.[3] First, Afro-American has a much older and more distinguished lineage within the black community than the more recent African-American. Second, Afro-American, in contrast to African-American, seems to us to emphasize more the uniquely American aspects of the black experience, an experience that has been a defining quality of America's core culture in a way that Africa has never been. Finally, we are also perplexed about what to call an immigrant from Africa to the United States, if not an African-American. Still, we are reminded of Carter G. Woodson's admonition in "Much Ado About a Name": "It does not matter so much what the thing is called as what the thing is."[4] We think the "thing" is the body of people who descended from African stock (readily acknowledging degrees of miscegenation) and were brought into this country and enslaved through the early decades of the nineteenth century. We expand on this in our discussion of Afro-Anglo culture as the core of American identity.

Our acknowledgments for this book are extensive and deep. We wish to extend our gratitude for support for the research for this book to the Twentieth Century Fund and the Ford and Rockefeller foundations. We especially want to thank Richard C. Leone, president of the Twentieth Century Fund, whose telephone call about doing a book on race relations in the armed forces came at precisely the time we were pondering such an undertaking. The Fund also provided continuing guidance throughout the writing of the book. We also wish to express our deep appreciation to William Diaz, then of the Ford Foundation, and Mary E. Rubin of the Rockefeller Foundation. We are enormously indebted to Kathleen A. Lynch and Paul Golob, who shared in many of the decisions in the editing of this book. We are also grateful to Chuck Cohen and Karen Feinberg, who were able to turn sociological jargon into readable prose. For critical readings of the manuscript we are especially indebted to F. William Smullen III, Thomas E. Ricks, and Peter C. Moskos. We would also like to thank Robert O. Woodson of the National Center for Neighborhood Enterprise for supporting our work.

Our ongoing access to soldiers was made possible by the personal interest in our work taken by four successive chiefs of staff of the U.S. Army: Edward C. Meyer, Carl T. Vuono, Gordon R. Sullivan, and Dennis J. Reimer. We also wish to acknowledge the longtime support of the deputy chief of staff for personnel, Lieutenant General Theodore G. Stroup, Jr.

Charles Moskos is deeply indebted to two individuals who collaborated in the collection of field data during the term of General Sullivan (1991–95). Major Angela Manos, Ph.D., a social scientist in her own right, was able to make things happen to suit the needs of the moment under amazingly different conditions, including zones of hostile fire.

Laura L. Miller, now Ph.D., then technically a student but really a colleague, was responsible for the construction, collection, and analysis of the survey data. Her wry humor and insights always lightened what were sometimes arduous research environments.

Many people helped out in the collection of the materials covered in this book, and we have departed from normal practice by citing them in the text or in appropriate endnotes in order to recognize their specific help. For opening doors for us and making certain data available we are indebted to John P. Abizaid, Katherine Barker, Hubert Bridges, F. Rick Brown, Harvey R. Gerry, Suzanne Goldsmith, Fred A. Gorden, David W. Grissmer, Ronald M. Joe, James M. Lyle, Charles W. McClain, David Meade, Milton D. Morris, Jack Muhlenbeck, Fred Peck, Donald L. Scott, W. Steve Sellman, John Shannon, Patrick A. Toffler, Steven Waldman, John Wattendorf, and Leonard Wong. Our gratitude is especially strong to Edwin Dorn, who encouraged this project both as a scholar and as an under secretary of defense.

Through numerous discussions on matters military-sociological, many people have contributed to our thoughts: R. W. Apple, Bernard Beck, Wendell Bell, Richard Berhenausen, Peter Braestrup, John Campbell, Neal Creighton, Michael Drillings, Jack Fuller, Alan L. Gropman, Samuel P. Huntington, Michael Kaplan, Edgar M. Johnson, Peter Marudas, Newton N. Minow, Aldon Morris, Joseph S. Nye, Jr., Robert E. Philips, Hugh Price, Jeff Rice, Elihu Rose, Zita Simutis, Bernard Trainor, and Samuel F. Wells, Jr.

We have profited greatly from discussions with many Army officers (active and retired) and wish to single out the following: Steven L. Arnold, Wallace C. Arnold, Julius W. Becton, Charles Bussey, Thomas P. Carney, Andrew Chambers, Wesley K. Clark, Tom Cuthbert, James M. Dubik, Samuel Ebbesen, John Fugh, Robert Gifford, William W. Hartzog, William Hauser, W. Daryl Henderson, Charles

Hines, Thomas C. Jones, Robert P. Kane, Gary Luck, Barry R. McCaffrey, Steven R. Mirr, William H. Reno, Michael Shaler, John M. Shalikashvili, Michael Sherfield, Thomas F. Sikora, Kenneth W. Simpson, Billy K. Solomon, Jr., and the late Roscoe Robinson. Most especially, we wish to recognize the intellectual guidance of Maxwell R. Thurman (1931–95), who turned the all-volunteer force around through use of social scientists to inform Army policy.

Charles Moskos would also like to acknowledge the Woodrow Wilson International Center for Scholars, the John Simon Guggenheim Foundation, and the Robert R. McCormick Tribune Foundation, whose support at different times gave him the opportunity to develop many of the materials that came to be included in this volume.

John Butler would like to thank the individuals and organizations that supported his research over the years and that laid the groundwork for many of the ideas presented here: William Alpert of the Donner Foundation, George Kozmetsky of the IC Institute at the University of Texas, and the Research Institute at the University of Texas.

Both of us also gratefully acknowledge the support of the U.S. Army Research Institute for the Behavioral and Social Sciences for our ongoing studies of the American soldier and racial issues. This unique organization is a lineal descendant from the Army research group that was established by George C. Marshall in World War II. It has consistently shown that doing good for the Army and doing good social research can be one and the same.

Much of our professional and intellectual life centers on the Inter-University Seminar on Armed Forces and Society, an "invisible college" of scholars founded by Morris Janowitz in 1960. The seminar served as the intellectual incubator for our thoughts on race relations in the military. We wish to thank especially the following seminar colleagues: James Burk, Paul Gade, Robert Goldich, Irving Louis

Horowitz, John Mearsheimer, Sam Sarkesian, Larry Seaquist, David R. Segal, Mady Wechsler Segal, H. Wallace Sinaiko, Sandra Stanley, Cynthia Watson, John A. Williams, and Chip Wood.

Finally, because parts of this book are likely to be controversial—at least we hope so—the usual caveat is especially relevant: that the authors alone are responsible for the findings and interpretation presented here.

C.C.M.   *J.S.B.*

Evanston, Illinois   *Austin, Texas*

FEBRUARY 1996

All That We Can Be

1

Success Story—With Caveats

Two tendencies dominate the way race is talked about in America. One emphasizes the ways blacks and whites exist in nearly complete isolation from each other, even inhabiting "two nations."[1] The other is to subsume the issue of race into the less sensitive realm of class. Underlying both ways of discussing race is the paradigm of black failure. That commentators attribute this failure to a diverse array of causes—white racism, black family breakdown, cultural differences, economic changes, public policy, and so on—does not change the relentlessly negative picture of black America that is the premise for most racial discussion in these waning years of the twentieth century.

One major American institution, however, contradicts the

prevailing race paradigm. It is an organization unmatched in its level of racial integration. It is an institution unmatched in its broad record of black achievement.[2] It is a world in which the Afro-American heritage is part and parcel of the institutional culture. It is the only place in American life where whites are routinely bossed around by blacks. The institution is the U.S. Army.

A visitor to an Army dining facility (as the old "mess hall" has been renamed) is likely to see a sight rarely encountered elsewhere in American life: blacks and whites commingling and socializing by choice. This stands in stark contrast to the self-imposed racial segregation in most university dining halls today—not to mention within most other locales in our society. In the Army whites and blacks not only inhabit the same barracks but also patronize equally such nonduty facilities as barber shops, post exchanges, libraries, movie theaters, and snack bars. And, in the course of their military duties, blacks and whites work together with little display of racial animosity. Give or take a surly remark here, a bruised sensibility there, the races get on remarkably well.

As a rule of thumb, the more military the environment, the more complete the integration. Interracial comity is stronger in the field than in garrison, stronger on duty than off, stronger on post than in the world beyond the base. Even in the grueling conditions of deployments to the Persian Gulf, Somalia, or Haiti, not a single racial incident occurred that was severe enough to come to the attention of the military police—not one.

Even off duty and off post, far more interracial mingling is noticeable around military bases than in civilian life. Most striking, the racial integration of military life has some carryover into the civilian sphere. The most racially integrated communities in America are towns with large military installations.[3] These include Fayetteville (Fort Bragg) and Jacksonville (Camp Lejeune) in North Carolina; Killeen (Fort

Hood), Texas; and Lawton (Fort Sill), Oklahoma. This is happening at a time when demographers and social analysts report increasing self-segregation of whites both in regional geography and in private residential communities.[4]

Consciousness of race in a nonracist organization is one of the defining qualities of Army life. The success of race relations and black achievement in the Army revolves around this paradox. A story several black soldiers told us at Fort Hood, Texas, may help illustrate this point. It seems that one table in the dining facility had become, in an exception to the rule, monopolized by black soldiers. In time, a white sergeant came over and told the blacks to sit at other tables with whites. The black soldiers resented the sergeant's rebuke. When queried, the black soldiers were quite firm that a white soldier could have joined their table, had one wished to do so. Why, the black soldiers wondered, should they have to take the initiative in integrating the dining tables?

This story has another remarkable point: that a white would take it upon himself to approach a table of blacks with that kind of instruction. The white sergeant's intention, however naive or misdirected, was to end a situation of racial self-segregation. Suppose a white professor asked black students at an all-black table in a college dining hall to sit at other tables with whites? This very question shows the contrast between race relations on campus and in the Army.

Good Race Relations, Not Perfect

In noting and celebrating the success of good race relations in the Army, we are not blind to real and serious problems that persist. The Army is not a racial utopia. Black and white soldiers are susceptible to the same kinds of interracial suspicion and resentment that exist in civilian society.

Although the Army stands in sharp and favorable contrast to nonmilitary institutions, it is not immune to the demons that haunt race relations in America.

A particularly alarming incident occurred in December 1995, when two white soldiers stationed at Fort Bragg murdered a black couple on the streets of Fayetteville. The killings were clearly racially motivated, and local police found Nazi flags and racist literature in the off-post mobile home of one of the soldiers. Though characterized as an isolated incident, Army officials immediately began an investigation to see if there were any patterns of white supremacist activity among soldiers, not only at Fort Bragg but also elsewhere in the Army. According to preliminary findings, no organized extremist right-wing groups were found to exist in the military, but anecdotal evidence also suggested that small numbers of soldiers could have become involved in such groups.[5]

The presence in the Army of white racist "skinheads," even if only a few, points to a profound and counterintuitive lesson. The Army has focused foremost on avenues that promote black achievement rather than on the rhetoric of nonracism, the aim being to maximize the avenues of opportunity as well as to combat overt and covert racism. But when these two goals come into conflict, the Army has deemed it better to have blacks in substantial numbers and in leadership positions in an organization with some white racists than to have an organization with few blacks and fewer black leaders where racial bigots are absent (or, more likely, invisible).

If a trade-off must be made between, on one side, black advancement coexisting with white racists and, on the other, few blacks in a putatively nonracial setting, the Army firmly comes down on the side of the former—in contrast to the state of affairs at most elite universities, where antiracism is promulgated but where the Afro-American presence is limited. The absence of white racists thus is not considered a precondition for black achievement.

How do whites and blacks perceive the racial climate in the military?[6] As in virtually all areas of American life, in the Army blacks see more racial discrimination than whites, but differences in perception are much smaller in the Army than in civilian life. Black soldiers are twice as likely as whites to discern racial discrimination in the Army.[7] Whites are not only less likely to see it, but when they do, they also see it as reverse discrimination. Even so, blacks are three times more likely to say that race relations are better in the Army than in civilian life. Whites are five times more likely to say so. Black career soldiers are also somewhat more likely (83 percent) than white career soldiers (73 percent) to express satisfaction with their Army career.[8] In a very revealing pattern, a study of military veterans found that almost twice as many black veterans (69 percent) as white (37 percent) wished they had stayed in the Army.[9]

A 1994 report of the House Armed Services Committee reiterated the disparate readings by blacks and whites on race relations. Though reporting an absence of overt racism in the military, the committee found continuing "subtle forms of racism" that affected minority career advancement and disciplinary actions as well as perception of reverse discrimination by whites.[10] And yet the methodology used in the House report was problematic, for the people interviewed were volunteers who had responded to publicity in advance of the committee staff's visit to military installations. This screening method almost guaranteed a negative bias—people with a bone to pick are likely to see such visits as a forum for airing their grievances. In light of the self-selection of the individual interviewees, the mildness of the committee's assessment of racial discrimination may be the report's most notable feature.

Still, whatever its racial tensions, the Army stands out,

even among governmental agencies, as an organization in which blacks often do better than their white counterparts. Here is a surprising statistic. Despite the federal government's strong commitment to establishing a good environment for racial minorities, black civil service employees are nearly two and a half times more likely to be fired than whites.[11] In the Army black soldiers are 20 percent less likely to be fired ("involuntarily separated") than white soldiers.[12]

Any discussion of race in the military must be placed in context. The most common topics of concern and conversation among and between blacks and whites have nothing to do with race, but deal with the work of the Army and with the good and the bad of military life. Friction in the Army arises not so much between the races as between lower-ranking soldiers and sergeants, between enlisted men and officers, between line units and staff units.

Why Study the Army?

We focus on the Army because it is the largest of the services and the one with by far the highest proportion of blacks. As of 1995, the 145,000 blacks in the Army constitute about half of all blacks in military uniform, as shown in table 1.1. Afro-Americans make up 27 percent of all Army personnel on active duty—about double the proportion in the Navy, Air Force, or Marine Corps. By rank, the number of blacks in the Army divides as follows: 24 percent of the lower enlisted levels, 35 percent of noncommissioned officers, and 12 percent of commissioned officers. Relative to the other military services, the Army stands out in the absolute and proportionate numbers of blacks at all levels, especially in the senior noncommissioned officer (NCO) and officer levels.

The large number of blacks in the Army has caused a "peacetime benefits versus wartime burdens" dilemma, in

TABLE 1.1

Blacks in the Armed Forces, 1995
(Percentage of All Personnel)

Grade	Army	Navy	Air Force	Marine Corps
Commissioned officers				
O–7 and above (generals)	7.3	2.2	2.6	0
O–6 (colonel)	5.2	1.8	2.1	3.2
O–5 (lieutenant colonel)	8.6	3.6	5.4	3.9
O–4 (major)	12.8	3.9	7.0	3.9
O–3 (captain)	12.5	5.5	5.5	4.8
O–2 (first lieutenant)	11.2	6.2	5.5	5.5
O–1 (second lieutenant)	10.7	8.7	5.1	6.8
Warrant officers	12.1	11.5	n/a	11.7
Total officers	11.4	5.4	5.6	5.6
Enlisted ranks				
E–9 (sergeant major)	28.3	6.6	15.8	23.5
E–8 (master sergeant)	32.1	8.2	18.3	23.5
E–7 (sergeant first class)	36.6	10.4	19.0	25.5
E–6 (staff sergeant)	38.2	15.4	18.7	27.0
E–5 (sergeant)	35.4	20.4	19.6	23.1
E–4 (corporal/specialist)	26.4	21.0	14.8	13.6
E–3 (private first class)	23.5	20.0	13.1	13.3
E–2 (private)	22.0	19.2	14.1	14.2
E–1 (private recruit)	24.3	21.7	17.0	13.6
Total enlisted	30.3	18.4	16.8	17.1
Total personnel	27.2	16.6	15.9	14.7

n/a = not applicable.
Note: Army titles given in parentheses have equivalent pay grades in other services.
Source: Defense Department.

the words of Martin Binkin and Mark Eitelberg.[13] In times of war, the presence of disproportionate numbers of blacks in the Army is seen as inflicting high casualties on America's most victimized group. In times of peace, these numbers are viewed as a source of opportunity for Afro-Americans. These benefits go beyond simple employment: an analysis of mortality rates shows that black soldiers die at half the rate of their age counterparts in civilian society. The most striking difference, by cause, is the markedly lower homicide death rate for black Army men. The homicide rate for blacks is an astounding twelve times higher in civilian life than in the Army.[14]

For many years, critics of heavy black representation in the Army have claimed that Afro-Americans have been used by their country as cannon fodder, an argument that had incredible emotional resonance during the Vietnam War. We have conducted a thorough analysis of Vietnam casualty rates and can report definitively that this charge is untrue (see table 1.2). Black fatalities amounted to 12.1 percent of all Americans killed in Southeast Asia—a figure proportional to the number of blacks in the U.S. population at the time and slightly lower than the proportion of blacks in the Army at the close of the war.

Table 1.2 also shows racial data, for the first time in print, on the combat deaths of American soldiers in the six combat operations since the end of the Vietnam War—Mayaguez, Lebanon, Grenada, Panama, the Gulf War, and Somalia.

TABLE 1.2

Blacks Killed in Action Since Vietnam

Military Operation	Total Killed	Blacks Killed	Blacks as Percentage of Total Killed
Mayaguez (1975)	14	1	7.1
Lebanon (1983)	254	46	18.1
Grenada (1983)	18	0	0
Panama (1989)	23	1	4.3
Gulf War (1991)	182	28	15.4
Somalia (1992–93)	29	2	6.9
Total	520	78	15.0

Notes:

a. Blacks comprised 12.1 percent of 47,193 combat deaths in the Vietnam War.

b. Blacks are 13.1 percent of 20–34-year-old U.S. population in 1990.

c. Blacks averaged 19.1 percent of active-duty military personnel, 1975–95.

Blacks account for 15 percent of combat deaths in these operations. This figure is slightly higher than that for the civilian black population of the relevant age group (13.1 percent), though somewhat lower than the percentage of blacks in the active-duty military (19.1 percent). No serious case can be made that blacks suffer undue casualties in America's wars and military interventions.

In this book, we examine some of the ways in which the Army's experience—and the Army's core principles—in the area of race relations can be transferred to the civilian sector, despite some obvious and important differences between the Army and nonmilitary organizations. One key difference between the way the Army and many civilian organizations reflect racial climate is that an officer's failure to maintain a bias-free environment is an absolute impediment to advancement in a military career. Most soldiers we have spoken to could not conceive of an officer who expressed racist views being promoted. We know of many civilian organizations in which this is not true.

Another, perhaps more important, distinction is that the Army does not lower its standards in order to assure an acceptable racial mix. When necessary, the Army makes an effort to compensate for educational or skill deficiencies by providing specialized, remedial training. Affirmative action exists, but without timetables or quotas governing promotions. What goals do exist are pegged to the proportion of blacks in the service promotion pool. Even then, these goals can be bypassed if the candidates do not meet standards.

In this regard, compared to most private organizations, the Army has an obvious advantage. The Army can maintain standards while still promoting Afro-Americans at all levels because of the large number of black personnel within the organization. The Army's experience with a plenitude of qualified black personnel illuminates an important lesson. When not marginalized, Afro-American cultural patterns can mesh with and add to the effectiveness of mainstream orga- nizations. The overarching point is that the most effective and fairest way to achieve racial equality of opportunity in the United States is to increase the number of qualified Afro- Americans available to fill positions. Doing so is no small task. But as an objective and basic principle, it is infinitely superior to a system under which blacks in visible positions of authority are presumed to have benefited from relaxed standards, a perception that stokes white resentment.

The notion that Afro-Americans cannot succeed without lowering standards is built on the paradigm of black failure. The goal of eliminating that paradigm is one all decent Americans should share, regardless of their political orienta- tion. To move toward that goal is the purpose of this book.

Can We Really Draw Lessons from the Army?

Even if we grant that racial integration and black achieve- ment have progressed further in the Army than in any other institution, can any lessons be drawn for civilian life? Surely the differences in formal organization and culture are so great, say the doubters, that little can be applied from the Army to the larger society. Critics might make three argu- ments to disqualify the Army as a model:

- The Army commands methods of surveillance and coer- cion unavailable to civilian institutions.

- Every individual in the Army has a modicum of eco- nomic security as well as decent housing and medical benefits for his or her family.

- Soldiers come from a segment of society that excludes the very bottom rungs; thus, they do not bring the most severe social problems into the Army.

In responding to these objections, we do not deny the significant differences between military and civilian life. Instead, we argue that the Army's ability to change its own way of doing things has broadly applicable implications for overcoming racism in America.

The Army is not a democracy—but neither are most other organizations. To be sure, the Army relies more strongly on round-the-clock accountability than most civilian organizations, but accountability and control cannot in and of themselves force good race relations. The racial situation is far worse in prisons, where coercive authority weighs much more heavily than in the military. Moreover, racist norms and behavior can prevail in any large organization, including those with quasi-military structures. We need only mention the raw racist words on tape of retired Los Angeles police detective Mark Fuhrman in connection with the O. J. Simpson trial and the continuing controversies over racism in local police departments. Even more telling were the racist signs and paraphernalia at the annual "Good Ol' Boys Roundup," a Tennessee gathering of federal law-enforcement officials and others from around the country.[15]

A more definitive rejoinder can be made to critics who state that the unique hierarchical conditions of military service account for its positive race relations. We must remember that the same authority structure existed in the Army of the 1970s, when racial turbulence was endemic. Something other than submersion of individual rights must have been involved in the Army's move from a racially tense situation to the relative harmony of the present period.

Concerning the second objection, it is true that soldiers enjoy some modicum of economic well-being. Once in the Army, not even the lowest soldier is "underclass." A private receives base pay of $10,000 a year, in addition to room and board, medical care, and other benefits. A master sergeant earns about $40,000 plus medical benefits for himself and his family, and is eligible for a pension of half of base pay after twenty years' service. A mid-level officer has similar benefits with base pay of about $55,000 a year. Again, however, we must ask why the Army of the 1970s was so torn by racial strife, when real earnings and benefits were practically identical to what they are today. Likewise, why are race relations generally better in the Army than in the other services, which all have nearly identical systems of authority and compensation?

The solid economic status of most soldiers does not explain the dynamics of race relations in the Army. After all, racial tensions have sharpened in society at large at all income levels. Indeed, the "rage" of the black middle class in a racist American society is an increasingly dominant theme in the current literature.[16]

The most salient objection to the Army as a model for race relations is the one least likely to be mentioned: the Army, while excluding the very bottom rungs of American society, does not recruit from America's elite youths either. Perhaps the reason for the silence on a broadly based sharing of duty is that it raises the specter of restoring the draft. In any event, as measured by test scores and school credentials, the Army effectively excludes the bottom third of black youths and the bottom fourth of white youths. This is a valid point and must be addressed seriously. After all, if it is simply the quality of youth that matters, then all the Army's racial experiences and equal opportunity programs are largely irrelevant.

The rebuttal to this argument is that race relations are better in the armed forces than in institutions that presumably recruit the highest-quality youths in America—our colleges and universities. By conventional standards, the quality of young people entering these leading universities far surpasses that of the Army recruits. Yet today, precisely when the U.S. Army is held up as a model of race relations, our campuses are divided by mutual racial isolation and, too often, by racial hostility. A sampling of newspaper headlines in the 1990s includes "Apartheid on Campus," "Campus Torn by Racial Strife," "Over 100 Arrested in Iowa Campus Brawl," and "On Once Liberal Campuses, Racial Divide Grows Wider."[17]

We have some pertinent data on this question. In 1993 we conducted a survey on racial attitudes among soldiers as well as among undergraduates at Northwestern University, a highly selective school with a fairly positive racial atmosphere. The soldiers, both black and white, were twice as likely to say they got along better with other races since joining the Army than were the students since arriving on campus. These data, to be more closely examined in chapter 6, should help put to rest that argument that the quality of recruits fully accounts for the Army's successful race relations.

In fact, anyone could easily trot out arguments to show why race relations should be worse in the Army than on campus. The Army, after all, is populated overwhelmingly by young males, the most trouble-prone group. The Army enforces constrained living conditions, with little outlet for private expression. Also, it sends young people into harm's way, a likelihood that should aggravate rather than reduce social tensions. How these negatives become positives are the key to the Army model.

What then can be learned? We suggest a broad lesson. Race relations can best be transformed by an absolute commitment to nondiscrimination, coupled with uncompromising standards of performance. To maintain standards, however, paths of opportunity must be created—through education, training, and mentoring—for individuals who otherwise would be at a disadvantage. We suggest another lesson as well: there must be enough blacks in the system. We do not know what the magic number is, but the lower range is probably close to the national ratio of one black for every nine Americans. This condition guarantees a sufficient pool from which to recruit black leaders, allows for the acceptance of features of Afro-American culture that enhance the organizational climate, and ensures that whites recognize the diversity among blacks.

Before turning to more specific lessons, let's first look at how the Army has treated black soldiers in the past and how they fare in the contemporary Army.

2

Blacks in the Common Defense

When William C. Nell, the pioneer black historian and abolitionist, was about to publish his book *Colored Patriots of the American Revolution* (1855), he asked his friend Harriet Beecher Stowe to write the introduction. As she tried to capture the significance of black soldiers and sailors who fought on the side of colonists, she noted: "We are to reflect upon them as far more magnanimous," because they served "a nation which did not acknowledge them as citizens and equals, and in whose interests and prosperity they had less at stake. . . . Bravery, under such circumstances, has a peculiar beauty and merit."[1]

Afro-American participation in the military has a noble and distinctive history no other racial or ethnic group can match. Afro-Americans grew up with America and have been a part of all of our conflicts and wars.[2] But the desire of blacks to serve their country, even when basic rights were denied, conflicted with the reality of slavery and the place of a slave in a democracy. Ever since that day, in the summer of 1619, when twenty kidnapped Africans were dragged onto American soil, the slaves had toiled in their chains. Conversely, the history of blacks in the military has always been associated with freedom and a degree of economic stability.

Segregation: From the Colonial Militia to World War II

Blacks participated as militiamen in the colonial era. In the Northern colonies, the lure of freedom brought many slaves into militia service, while free blacks joined as a way of raising themselves through military service. Blacks occasionally were allowed into Southern militias, but usually not in positions that entailed bearing arms. But whether in the North or in the South, the practice of using Afro-Americans in times of crisis and taking away their arms in times of peace set the stage for black participation in the military for years to come.

The Province of South Carolina typified the Southern system of using blacks in the military during the colonial era. In the early years of the eighteenth century, the colonists faced a hostile Indian population, and as the slave population began to exceed the number of free white citizens, the colony laid plans to arm certain slaves in case of war with the Yamassee Indian tribe. An Act of the General Assembly of the Province of South Carolina, December 23, 1703, became one of the first laws that made it possible, "for the safety of this colony," for a slave to bear arms:[3]

[I]t shall and may be lawful for any master or owner of any slave, in actual invasion, to arm and equip any slave or slaves, with such arms and ammunition as any other person by the act of militia are appointed to appear at muster or alarms.[4]

As a reward for killing or capturing an enemy during battle, the slave would "have and enjoy his freedom . . . ; and the master or owner of such slave [would] be paid and satisfied by the public."[5]

In 1715, the war with the Yamassees became a reality, and some slaves were given arms and received freedom in return for taking part in the campaign. (Similarly, in the French colony of Louisiana, slaves were enlisted to help defeat the Chickasaw and Natchez tribes.) During these conflicts, Afro-Americans served as soldiers, scouts, wagoners, laborers, and servants.[6] The Province of South Carolina also had plans to use slave manpower against a threatened Spanish invasion, but a slave uprising in 1739 persuaded officials that raising soldiers by this method was dangerous.

The crux of the issue in the arming of slaves was based on the simple notion that slave revolts would not only upset the white colonists' economic security and way of life but also reverse the fortunes of blacks and whites. In the case of South Carolina, the reason for revoking the 1703 law has become a classic statement in the history of blacks in the military: "There must be a great caution used, lest our slaves, when arm'd, become our masters."[7]

On a fall day in 1750, a quarter of a century before the Declaration of Independence, a slave from Massachusetts named Crispus Attucks struck a blow for his own liberty. The *Boston Gazette* ran the story on October 2, 1750:

Ran away from his Master William Brown of Framingham . . . a Mulatto Fellow, about 27 Years of age, named Crispas [sic] 6 feet two Inches high, short curl'd Hair,

his Knees nearer together than common; had on a light
colour'd Bearskin Coat.[8]

Although a bounty of ten pounds was placed on his head,
Attucks was never captured. His name again appeared in
print twenty years later when he became the first martyr of
the American Revolution, in an incident that has come to be
known as the Boston Massacre.

During these years, free Afro-Americans were developing
in Philadelphia one of the new world's most successful business communities. One of those young entrepreneurs, James
Forten, was destined to succeed handsomely by developing a
company that manufactured sails for seagoing vessels.[9] When
war came in 1775, these Afro-Americans dropped their ven-
tures and answered the call to serve in the Continental Army.

Despite the actions of free Afro-Americans, and the significance of the Attucks incident, when the Revolutionary War
began General George Washington's headquarters issued four
orders forbidding Afro-American enlistment in the Continental Army. This action barred from service thousands of
slaves and black freemen who were willing to bear arms on
behalf of the colonies. This exclusion was the decision of the
Colonial Counsel of Generals, many of whom were from the
plantation colonies.

In response, the British offered Afro-Americans their freedom if they would join the side of the Crown, and many
slaves did join the side of England. As Benjamin Quarles
explains in *The Negro in the American Revolution*, the black
soldier in the Revolutionary War

> can best be understood by realizing that his major loy-
> alty was not to a place nor a people, but to a princi-
> ple. . . . He was likely to join the side that made him the
> quickest and best offer in terms of those "unalienable
> rights" of which Mr. Jefferson had spoken.[10]

Had the British bid for black soldiers succeeded in recruiting large numbers, the colonists' goal of independence might never have been realized. When their plans reached General Washington, he issued an order authorizing recruiting officers to accept free blacks into the ranks of the Continental Army. In a letter to the Continental Congress, Washington wrote:

It has been presented to me, that the free Negroes, who have served in the past, are very dissatisfied at being discarded. As it is to be apprehended, that they may seek employment in the Ministerial Army, I have . . . given license for their being enlisted. If this is disapproved by Congress, I will put a stop to it.[11]

Congress did not disapprove Washington's actions, and Afro-Americans were allowed to enlist officially in the Continental Army, with only Georgia and South Carolina refusing to accept black enlistment. The presence of black soldiers, not surprisingly, raised a great deal of conflict between Northern and Southern colonies. Brigadier General John Thomas felt compelled to advise John Adams on October 24, 1775:

I am sorry to hear that any prejudice should take place in any of the southern colonies with respect to the troops raised in this; . . . The regiments at Roxbury, the privates are equal to any that I served with in the last war . . . we have some Negroes, but I look on them in general equally serviceable with other men, for fatigue and in action.[12]

More than 5,000 blacks, including James Forten and his fellow Philadelphians, served in the Revolutionary War.[13] The ranks were integrated. The typical Afro-American soldier was a private, often lacking a name and official identity. He was carried on the rolls as "A Negro man," or "negro by name," or "A Negro name not Known."[14]

As the war wore on, Afro-Americans enlisted freely, many slaves serving in place of their masters. The seven brigades of Washington's army averaged 54 blacks each. Pressed by Congress to raise troops, Rhode Island in 1778 paid owners up to 120 pounds a slave, and gave slaves their freedom in return for service. Massachusetts had two black companies, the Massoit Guards and the Bucks of America.[15] At Concord and at Lexington, black and white men stood shoulder to shoulder, and blacks were present at the battles of Saratoga, Red Bank, Princeton, Savannah, Monmouth, Bunker Hill, White Plains, and Long Island.

Once the British forces had been defeated and liberties secured, Afro-Americans were again excluded from military service. The ideology of war, the promises of freedom by the Army, were replaced by the conservatism of the constitutional era. The aftermath of the racial reality of the war was summarized by John Greenleaf Whittier, poet laureate of antislavery, at a July Fourth celebration in 1874:

> The return of the festival of our national independence has called our attention to a matter which has been carefully kept out of sight by orators and toast-drinkers. We allude to the participation of colored men in the great struggle for freedom. . . . Of the services and suffering of the colored soldiers of the Revolution, no attempt has been made, to our knowledge, to preserve a record. They have no historian. . . . Yet enough is known to show that the free colored men of the United States bore their full proportion of the sacrifices and trials of the Revolutionary War.[16]

The participation of Afro-Americans in defense forces prior to and during the Revolutionary War is testimony to the historical bridge with military institutions. Their experiences and blood thus pervade the very foundation of America.

The War of 1812 again brought a need for manpower. Although blacks officially were excluded, at least 3,000 black soldiers and sailors saw service in that conflict. They served in often de facto integrated military units, especially aboard ships in the new American Navy.

The Civil War struck at the roots of slaveholder power, and Afro-Americans were among the most fervent supporters of the Union cause. When Northern blacks enthusiastically responded to the first call for volunteers, however, the Secretary of War said bluntly, "This department has no intention to call into service any colored soldiers."[17] This rejection would be reversed as the Civil War created the greatest manpower shortage that the military had seen.

This rejection of Afro-American troops was based on the assumption that white volunteers would suffice to defeat the South. Ideological differences about the place of slavery during the conflict were also visible within the Union Army. On the one hand, Major General John Fremont, commander of the Department of the West and an abolitionist, wished to punish Southerners by freeing slaves owned by secessionists as his troops marched South. On the other hand, Major General Thomas W. Sherman, commanding Union troops at Port Royal, South Carolina, promised that his forces would not disturb the "peculiar institution" of the South.[18]

The idea that blacks could not fight in the Civil War drew a patriotic response from Afro-Americans. After the fall of Fort Sumter, Northern blacks continued to offer their service. In a letter to the secretary of war, an Afro-American from Washington, D.C., wrote:

> Sir: I desire to inform you that I know of some three hundred of reliable colored free citizens of this City, who desire to enter the service for the defense of the City. I can be found about the Senate Chambers, as I have been employed about the premises for some years.[19]

In Pittsburgh the Hannibal Guards, an Afro-American organization, offered its services to General James S. Negley, militia commander of Western Pennsylvania:

> [A]s we consider ourselves American citizens and inter-
> ested in the Commonwealth of all our white fellow-
> citizens, although deprived of all our political rights,
> we yet wish the government of the United States to be
> sustained against the tyranny of slavery, and are willing
> to assist in any honorable way or manner to sustain the
> present administration.[20]

Afro-Americans were well aware of the history of their participation in the military during the colonial period. Early in the Civil War, a group of Boston blacks met in the Twelfth Baptist Church and called for a repeal of laws that kept them out of the Army. Robert Morris, a lawyer of the group, noted that "if the Government would only take away the disability, there was not a man who would not leap for his knapsack and musket, and they would make it intolera-bly hot for Old Virginia."[21] During the same time period, an Afro-American drill company was organized in Boston, and it sent petitions to the legislature seeking the repeal of dis-criminatory militia laws.

As Afro-Americans mounted protest after protest regard-ing service to country, they were constantly reminded that this was not their battle but a "white man's war." The admin-istration of President Abraham Lincoln and antislavery newspapers like the New York *Tribune* all pointed out that the purpose of the war was to restore the Union, and that the issue of ending slavery had nothing to do with it. The Spring-field *Republican* stated: "If there is one point of honor upon which more than another this administration will stick, it is its pledge not to interfere with slavery in the states."[22]

One of the earliest fighting units organized from former slaves was the First South Carolina Volunteers, formed in 1862.[23] But it was not until the Emancipation Proclamation came into effect in January 1863 that black soldiers were offi-cially allowed to enter the Union Army. Over 180,000 free blacks and former slaves fought on the side of the Union, and were formed into the separate units designated "United States Colored Troops."

Black units fought in pivotal battles, won fourteen Con-gressional Medals of Honor, and played major roles in the liberation of Petersburg and Richmond.[24] Their casualty rate was 40 percent higher than the white rate, but until 1865, all blacks were paid half as much, $7 a month against $13 a month for the lowest-ranking white.[25]

One of the most memorable units of the Civil War was the 54th Massachusetts Regiment, formed in 1863, whose saga was recounted in the movie *Glory* (1992). Raised by Colonel Robert Gould Shaw, the 54th was recruited from liberated slaves. The unit entered history in the assault to capture Bat-tery Wagner near Charleston, South Carolina. In one of the most withering battles of the Civil War, half of the officers and men of the 54th Regiment were killed or wounded, including Shaw. The Confederates' hatred of any white offi-cer who would lead black troops was so deep that Shaw's body was thrown into a mass grave upon which dead black troops were heaped.

During Reconstruction, the Republican Party argued that "blacks in blue" should be integrated into the regular mili-tary establishment of the United States with all basic politi-cal rights,[26] but this integration was not achieved. Instead, the Congress created six Army regiments of Afro-American troops, two cavalry and four infantry. Even so, this legisla-tion opened a new chapter in American military history, for it also allowed the former slaves to play a major role in the settlement of the country as it moved west.

The black 9th and 10th Cavalry Regiments, commanded by white officers, had the duty of controlling hostile Indians on the Great Plains, a job that they did for over twenty years.

Because of their fierce nature and the texture of their hair, the Indians called them "buffalo soldiers." Operating under the extreme conditions of the West, the buffalo soldiers not only had to fight off Indians but also had to contend with the hostility of the settlers they were protecting. As noted by the historian William H. Leckie, "The Ninth and Tenth Cavalry were first-rate regiments and major forces in promoting peace and advancing civilization along America's last continental frontier."[27]

In June 1898, Afro-Americans again responded to the call to arms to fight, this time on Cuban soil. One of the most publicized events of the Spanish-American War was Teddy Roosevelt's victorious charge up San Juan Hill and the bravery of the Afro-American troops who assisted as "Rough Riders." At El Caney, black troops won high praise for bravery when, under heavy fire, they stormed a stone fort defended by Spanish troops. Later, Roosevelt wrote, "I want no better men beside me in battle than these colored troops showed themselves to be."[28]

Despite their outstanding performance in Cuba, blacks at home were increasingly terrorized by night riders, mainly, though not exclusively, in the South. At the turn of the twentieth century, lynchings averaged close to two hundred annually. In cities, antiblack riots occurred with more frequency. An outbreak of violence in Brownsville, Texas, in 1906, had more than a few ironies. After being attacked by local whites, black soldiers, many of them veterans of the war with Spain, retaliated. Theodore Roosevelt, now president and the same man who once had nothing but praise for black soldiers, dismissed three companies of black troops with dishonorable discharges—all without investigation. Not until 1972 was this decision reversed.

The years preceding World War I saw a continued worsening of race relations in American society. President Woodrow Wilson ordered the segregation of federal employees in the nation's capital. In 1915 alone 69 blacks were lynched in the

United States. Yet despite these events, when the United States declared war on Germany in the spring of 1917, Afro-American leaders urged blacks to support Wilson's call to "Make the World Safe for Democracy." At the same time, Representative Frank Park (D-Ga.) introduced a bill to make it unlawful to appoint blacks to the rank of either noncommissioned or commissioned officers.[29] Though the Army systematically denied the participation of blacks, it did make certain concessions. A letter sent to an Atlanta magazine in 1917 captures the essence of the military as a place of black opportunity:

> A reserve officers' training camp, accommodating 1,250, at Des Moines, Iowa, for colored men, to start June 15. . . . Stop but a moment, brother, and realize what this means. At present, we have only three officers of the line in the army; in less than four months we shall have 1,250 officers. Our due recognition at last. . . . [T]he Negro has had no chance to fight under his own leadership. Now the chance has come; the first opportunity since the Civil War.[30]

During this time period, newly formed civil rights organizations clearly distinguished the problems of race at home from the problems of race that could develop if Germany won the war. W. E. B. Du Bois, a founder of the NAACP and editor of its official newspaper, *The Crisis*, noted:

> We of the colored race have no ordinary interest in the outcome. That which the German power represents today spells death to the aspirations of Negroes and all darker races for equality, freedom, and democracy. Let us not hesitate. Let us, while this war lasts, forget our special grievances and close our ranks shoulder to shoulder with our own white fellow citizens and the allied nations that are fighting for democracy.[31]

In a little-known footnote to Afro-American history, Du Bois considered accepting a commission in the U.S. Army during World War I. Eventually, he did go to France, where he documented the ill-treatment of black soldiers by their American commanders. Du Bois, of course, was an epochal figure in American history, who in his last years moved to Ghana, renounced his American citizenship, and converted to communism on his deathbed. When he was pondering the Army commission, however, he came "nearer to feeling myself a real and full American than ever before or since."[32]

Afro-America, as evidenced by Martin Luther King, Jr.'s opposition to the Vietnam War, has also had a pacifist side.[33] Booker T. Washington, the most influential black leader from 1895 until his death in 1915, is conventionally looked upon as an accommodationist. Yet Washington's pacifist views were already evident in his opposition to both the Spanish-American War and World War I. It was the more radical Du Bois who, upon the U.S. entry into World War I, urged blacks to participate in the war effort in the armed services and at home.

Some 380,000 Afro-Americans served in World War I, 42,000 of them in combat units. The large majority served as laborers in engineer, quartermaster, and other service battalions. Again, the pattern was one of initial resistance to using black troops, followed by widespread use in the face of manpower shortages.

During the war, the performance of two black divisions, the 92nd and the 93rd, produced conflicting versions of this familiar story. Both were led by black officers in the junior grades and white officers at the senior levels. Even while the 92nd was in training, black leaders became suspicious of the Army's intentions. Du Bois, writing in *The Crisis*, maintained that the division was headed for failure because the white officer corps, mainly from the South, was viewed as particularly hostile to black subordinates. Du Bois's apprehensions were confirmed, as the division's combat performance in France was mixed at best. The 93rd was also sent to France, but with an entirely different experience. Serving under French command in a much more racially benign climate, the 93rd had such a distinguished battle record that the division was awarded the Croix de Guerre. The French command also asked the United States to send to France all the black units that could be spared.[34]

Between World Wars I and II, the Army remained segregated and adopted a quota system that kept the number of blacks in the Army proportionate to the total population. By 1940 only 5,000 men served in all-black units; of the five Afro-American officers, three were chaplains.[35]

At the outbreak of World War II, America turned again to its people of color for manpower, but World War I had left Afro-Americans deeply disillusioned. A number of black leaders envisioned history repeating itself. A. Philip Randolph, who headed the union of Pullman car porters, called for a march on Washington, D.C., to end official segregation in both civilian and military life:

> We call upon you to fight for jobs in National Defense. . . .
> We call upon you to struggle for the integration of Negroes in the Armed Forces. . . . This is the hour of crisis. . . . To American Negroes, it is the denial of jobs in Governmental defense projects. It is widespread Jim-Crowism in the Armed Forces of the nation.[36]

The effectiveness of Randolph and other black leaders would be measured after the war. During the war years, pressures for manpower were great, and concentration was placed on defeating a common enemy of the United States.

On September 27, 1940, the Army prepared a statement of policy that, with the approval of President Franklin Delano Roosevelt, became the official document for the treatment of Afro-American soldiers. Contained in a memorandum to the president from Assistant Secretary of War Robert P. Patterson, it was the military application of "separate but equal":

> [S]ervices of Negroes will be utilized on a fair and equi-
> table basis. . . . The policy of the War Department is not
> to intermingle colored and white enlisted personnel in
> the same regimental organizations. The policy has been
> proven satisfactory over a long period of years and to
> make changes would produce situations destructive to
> morale and detrimental to the preparations for national
> defense ... the department does not contemplate
> assigning colored reserve officers other than those of the
> Medical Corps and chaplains to existing Negro combat
> units of the regular army.[37]

As usual in times of manpower shortages, the Army
relaxed its restrictive race policies, and the segregated Army
grew again as units were reactivated and new ones were
formed. Some 2,500 blacks volunteered for the Battle of the
Bulge in the winter of 1944–45, serving in all-black platoons
within white companies. The black soldiers' excellent combat performance, coupled with a lack of serious friction from
white troops, made the experiment an unqualified success.[38]

In another precedent-breaking experiment on the race
relations front, the all-black 332nd Fighter Group, trained at
Tuskegee, Alabama, engaged in aerial combat over Italy and
escorted bombers deep into Germany.[39] Not one bomber
entrusted to the 332nd was lost to enemy fighters—a claim
no other unit could make. The "Tuskegee Airmen," whose
flying crews were black commissioned officers, were commanded by Benjamin O. Davis, Jr., who would later become
the first black to hold three-star rank.

In his memoirs, Davis recounts his days at West Point,
where he had been the first black to graduate in this century.
He was subjected to "silencing"; no cadet would speak to
him except in the course of duty.[40] Davis remembers every
insult and candidly admits preferring overseas assignments
and the more benign racial climate outside the United States.
At the same time, he remains devoted to the military, which

he sees as an honorable profession. And he believes that America, with all its faults, is worth dying for.

As for the role of black women in World War II, Mary McLeod Bethune, as a special assistant to the secretary of war, had a significant impact on women's issues in the military and in the establishment of the Women's Army Corps. She is a landmark figure in Afro-American history for her work in education and her high appointments in the New Deal administration of Franklin Delano Roosevelt. Brenda Moore has given us a vivid account of the only battalion of black women, a postal unit, to serve overseas.[41]

All told, more than a million blacks took part in World War II, about 10 percent of total military personnel. All of them served in segregated units, mostly in the Army. Some black combat units saw extensive action, but most blacks were employed in support roles. To make matters worse from the viewpoint of "the right to fight," a slogan echoed loudly at the time by civil rights organizations in the United States, even black combat units were used frequently for heavy labor.

Henry Louis Gates, Jr., makes the point that the Army of World War II may have created modern Afro-American culture. The military service of that period mixed the black culture that had developed in the cities of the North with the old black culture of the rural South.[42]

After World War II, under pressure from black and liberal white groups around the country, the military began to reexamine its use of black troops. An Army Board, headed by Lieutenant General Alvan C. Gillem, concluded in 1945 that, although racial integration was desirable, practical considerations of white resistance required maintenance of segregation and the quota system. It further recommended that black personnel be assigned exclusively to support units, not combat arms.

In the early spring of 1948, two black leaders paid a call on

President Harry S. Truman: A. Philip Randolph of the Brotherhood of Sleeping Car Porters and the Reverend Grant Reynolds of the Committee Against Jim Crow in Military Service and Training. Both threatened a campaign of civil disobedience if Truman did not abolish racial segregation in the Army. Truman was alert to the need to appeal to black voters in the forthcoming presidential election. He may also have been persuaded by the merits of racial integration as a principle.

Whatever the precise calculus of the president's motives, on July 26, 1948, Truman signed Executive Order 9381, the decisive desegregation order:

> It is the declared policy of the President of the United States that there shall be equality of treatment and opportunity for all persons in the Armed Forces. This policy shall be put into effect as rapidly as possible, having due regard to the time required to effectuate any necessary changes without impairing efficiency or morale.[43]

The order also established the President's Committee on Equality of Treatment and Opportunity, under Charles H. Fahy, to see that the new policy was carried out. The Fahy Committee, in 1950, abolished the quota system and pressured the Army to integrate its training camps.[44]

Organizational Integration, from Korea to Vietnam

Beginning with the Korean War in 1950, desegregation became the practice first on training bases in the United States, then in combat units in Korea, and finally on American military installations around the world. Truman's edict may have been due to good intentions as well as to political pressure from civil rights groups, but, with the outbreak of hostilities, the need for more effective use of military manpower became immediate.[45] In Korea, for the first time since the Revolutionary War, Afro-Americans and whites fought in formally integrated units. As integration in Korea became standard, commanders noted that there was no difference between the fighting abilities of Afro-Americans and whites.[46] Indeed, integrated units fought better than all-white or all-black units.

The armed forces were integrated in two phases. During the first phase, in the 1950s, *organizational integration* put an end to any formal discrimination in recruitment, training, retention, and on-base living arrangements. From the Pentagon's viewpoint, this was a quiet period in race relations. The second phase, *leadership integration*, would not occur for another quarter of a century. Truman's executive order had brought blacks part of the way into the military mainstream; the upheaval of the late 1960s gave the impetus for measures leading to full equality.

By the mid-1950s, a snapshot of a hundred enlisted men on a typical parade would have shown twelve black faces; integration had become a fact of Army life. At a time when Afro-Americans were still arguing for their educational rights before the Supreme Court and marching for their social and political rights in the Deep South, the Army had become desegregated with little fanfare. What the Army may have lost in support from some of its traditional conservative allies, it gained immeasurably from the black community.

Integration went so smoothly at the beginning partly because it affected only enlisted men, and enlisted men of every race had always been treated, as the saying went, "like Negroes." There were few black officers in the Army during the 1950s and even the 1960s, so integration required only minor adjustments on the part of the command structure. If the paucity of black officers (they would be a negligible number well into the Vietnam era) helped to facilitate integration in the early stages, it was also one obvious indication that opportunities for Afro-American leaders in the armed services were severely constrained.

After Korea, racial relations in the Army continued to improve. Peacetime Army personnel experienced the results of the Army's ongoing policy of integration. Many commentators viewed the military as engaged in a revolution as a result of allowing all Americans to defend the country. One comment, from the *Saturday Evening Post*, is typical:

> Tell one of the generals . . . that he and his brother brass are staging a social revolution among the half-million Americans posted to duty . . . and he will profess the greatest astonishment. . . . It may be a paradox that the staff planners of the . . . Army . . . refuse to recognize the dimensions of the task they are performing and that the very matter-of-factness of their approach has been a major factor in its success thus far . . . this "ordinary implementation of a routine directive" does add up to a revolution in race relations and appears to be setting a pattern not yet equalled elsewhere in our Armed Forces or anywhere in our country.[47]

The Vietnam War, however, heightened racial polarization in the armed forces. Many black leaders denounced the war, but the antiwar movement at home was led mainly by whites. Middle-class whites were the most adept at avoiding the draft, legally and illegally. Race relations worsened over the course of the war; those years were marked by well-publicized breakdowns of discipline among servicemen and, more broadly, by an atmosphere of racial hostility in the ranks. Racial clashes occurred in Vietnam, on military bases around the world, and on ships at sea. By the early 1970s, racial strife was widespread in the ranks, an outcome of both real and perceived discrimination against blacks in the military and spillover from the racial and political turmoil in society at large. This situation must be seen in context, however. In the waning years of the war, the Army was unraveling not only racially but also in many other ways—drug abuse, indiscipline, even "fraggings" (killings of superiors).

While the most emotional race issue of the Vietnam era—the purported disproportionate number of blacks being killed in the war—was not borne out by the facts, other issues were legitimate. Where was the black officer corps? To be sure, the black draftees of the 1950s were fast becoming senior noncommissioned officers, but as late as 1968 fewer than one in a hundred plebes starting West Point were black. At the end of the Vietnam War, only three in a hundred Army officers were black.

Phase Two: Leadership Integration, from Vietnam to Today's Army

Racial conflict did not disappear in 1973 with the end of the draft and the withdrawal from the Vietnam War. In many ways it grew worse. Fights between black and white soldiers were endemic in the 1970s, an era now remembered as the "time of troubles." The race problems of the early all-volunteer force (AVF) loomed so ominously because they could not be explained by the usual breakdown of discipline that occurs at the end of every war.

The AVF changed the demographics of the Army. In the last year of the draft, blacks made up about 17 percent of the enlisted force. By the late 1970s, that proportion had nearly doubled. With the advent of the volunteer military, the white middle-class enlisted man became an endangered species. Armed with bonuses and the prospect of good pay, the military turned into another competitor in the labor market, replacing the citizen-soldier with Economic Man. The results were disastrous. Not only had college-educated soldiers disappeared, but the Army also found recruits with even a high school diploma increasingly difficult to obtain. Army recruiters drew from the poorest and toughest elements of America, white and black. Drugs and hooliganism infested the barracks. Today's senior officers and noncoms remember the 1970s with even more dismay than the Vietnam years.

In the early 1980s, the military took a hard look at its enlistment procedures. Under the leadership of General Maxwell R. Thurman, recruitment policies were redirected away from enlistment bonuses toward an emphasis on postservice educational benefits. This development was capped by the Montgomery GI Bill in 1985. The new enlistment incentives turned the Army around. When AVF veterans are asked how important GI Bill benefits were in their enlistment decision, 51 percent of blacks (32 percent of whites) answer "important" or "very important."[48] It is also noteworthy that white and black soldiers take advantage of postservice educational benefits at the same rate, about 80 percent.[49] Indeed, the greatest long-term avenue of equal opportunity in American society may be the GI Bill benefits offered by the Army.

The most significant development of the 1970s was the increase in the number of black leaders in the Army. The number of black senior NCOs grew from 14 percent in 1970 to 26 percent in 1980 and to 31 percent in 1990, where it has stayed. Among commissioned officers, the proportion of blacks grew from 3 percent in 1970 to 7 percent in 1980 and to 11 percent in 1990. By the mid-1980s, blacks accounted for roughly 7 percent of all Army generals, and they still do. Integration of leadership brought the Army out of its "time of troubles." A most significant threshold was crossed in 1989 when Colin L. Powell was named chairman of the Joint Chiefs of Staff, the most powerful military position in the world.

The rise of blacks in Army leadership in the active-duty force was mirrored on the civilian side of the Army. The 1977 appointment of Clifford Alexander, a black, as secretary of the Army seemed to ratify what was occurring at all levels in that branch of the armed forces. Alexander introduced much of the leadership integration in the Army. Even in the Reagan administration, not known for its openness to blacks, the Department of the Army was an exception. John O. Marsh, Jr., a white secretary of the Army, was respected for his unusual sensitivity to racial matters, and he appointed blacks to two of the five assistant secretary positions: Delbert R. Spurlock, for manpower and reserve affairs, and John W. Shannon, for installations and logistics. In the Bush administration, Shannon served as undersecretary of the Army and, during the transition phase of the Clinton administration, as acting secretary of the Army. Also, in the Clinton administration, Edwin Dorn, a leading researcher on race relations in the military, became the undersecretary of defense for personnel and readiness. With the appointment of Togo West, Jr., as secretary of the Army in 1993, the presence of a black in the senior Army Secretariat had become almost the norm.

When Desert Shield/Desert Storm took place in 1990–91, racial integration of the military organization and leadership was complete. Over 500,000 American troops, 24 percent of them black, were sent to the Persian Gulf. For the Army, the figure was 30 percent black.[50] Indeed, the nature of race relations in the Gulf War had become such a nonstory that media attention shifted to the more topical issue of women in the military.

Perhaps the most telling example of race relations in the U.S. Army in recent years was Operation Restore Hope in Somalia during 1992–93. In all the second thoughts about U.S. action in Somalia, a major story was largely overlooked: it was the first major deployment of American troops to an African nation. The operation was successful, and the black troops served with distinction. In fact, the American forces were the only multiracial contingent in the United Nations force (and the only one to include women). For many black soldiers, this was an opportunity to perform a humanitarian mission on a continent to which they traced their roots, however distant. (The 1994 deployment of American troops to Haiti did not have the same resonance for black soldiers; the emotional symbolism of Africa far outweighed that of the black Caribbean.) In their reactions to the Somalis, whites and blacks differed, the latter being somewhat more empathetic.[51]

Yet the overriding finding was that the realities of Somalia disabused most black soldiers of romanticized, mythologized notions of Africa and African commonalities with Afro-Americans. Instead, the Somali experience brought home to many black soldiers just how different they were from Africans. A black sergeant major in an Army engineer battalion in Somalia said:

> I deployed as an American and I'll come back as an American. This talk about our ancestors coming from here has it wrong. My people are from East Texas. I learned a lot about race the hard way back home. But in the Army we should all be brothers in the same church.

In Mogadishu, Sergeant Michael Hartwell showed us a poem he had written, which he called "Africa":

> *Today, I stand where might my forefathers stood.*
> *I am here not because of history, but of duty.*
> *At last we meet and we stare.*
> *He's probably wondering the same thing I am.*
> *Or does he realize the difference, not of our clothes but*
> *of our milestones?*
> *He speaks to me in his native tongue, almost as though I*
> *should know.*
> *Sorry, my friend, I would reply, but due to history, I've*
> *lost our ties.*

3

Making It: Afro-Americans in Today's Army

An integrated military, with a just distribution of blacks throughout the ranks, should be a source of pride for a country whose national principles stress equality of opportunity. But the importance of the Army's experience is more than simply symbolic.

Throughout our history, military service has been a source of stable family life in black America. Money earned in military service has paid for the educations of generations of black children. Before the development of federal aid for college students, the Reserve Officers Training Corps (ROTC) at historically black colleges was the major federal governmental subsidy for higher education for black men. The experience of military service itself has taught young adults (black and white) valuable skills and life traits such as self-reliance and self-esteem. The record of blacks in today's Army—from private to general—is, in the main, one of extraordinary achievement.

Enlisted Ranks

The Army's enlisted members come disproportionately from the pool of young blacks and will continue to do so as long as opportunities for these youths remain limited in civilian life. A 1986 study by the Brookings Institution showed that 20 percent of black male youths participated in the military, compared with 13 percent of whites.[1] Among qualified youths—those who met the physical and mental standards—an astonishing 50 percent of all blacks joined the military, against only 16 percent of their white counterparts.[2]

Since the end of the draft, the proportion of high school graduates among blacks entering the Army has consistently exceeded that among whites. In the late 1970s, about nine in ten black Army recruits had high school diplomas, compared to four whites in ten. Indeed, the Army's enlisted ranks have been the only significant social arena where blacks' educational levels have surpassed those of whites, and, until recently, by quite a large margin. With the overall improvement in recruitment, the gap has narrowed: in 1994, 99 percent of black recruits and 97 percent of white recruits were high school graduates.

Young men and women can enlist in the Army for two, three, or four years. All soldiers undergo two months of physically demanding basic training. For many youths from impoverished neighborhoods, successful completion of basic training gives them their first chance to outshine their more privileged counterparts.

After basic training recruits are sent to advanced training and assignment to a military occupational specialty (MOS). Most advanced training courses take six to twelve weeks; training for some technical specialties may require as long as a year. Upon completion of advanced training, soldiers are sent to a permanent duty station, where most of them can expect to complete their initial enlistment.

Black and white soldiers diverge during selection for advanced training because black soldiers usually score lower than whites on military entrance tests. In 1994, for example, 83 percent of white recruits scored in the upper half of the mental aptitude test (compared with 61 percent of white youths in the national population), while 59 percent of black recruits scored in the upper half (compared with 14 percent of the black youths nationwide). Thus, although blacks' and whites' test scores are much closer among soldiers than among civilians, the gap is still wide.

Because scores on aptitude tests help to determine a soldier's MOS, a racial difference is present in many military jobs. Thus, blacks are more likely than whites to be assigned to combat "support" branches of the Army. Afro-Americans fill about half the jobs in supply, transportation, and food service. Blacks are less likely than whites to work in highly technical fields, accounting for only eleven jobs in a hundred in electronic warfare, for example. The disparities in job assignments stem ultimately from the fact that the Army is not totally insulated from civilian life. Blacks in the military are more likely than whites to have high school diplomas, but they are also more likely to have attended less effective public schools. The Army can often mitigate the effects of social and educational deprivation, but it cannot eliminate them.

Even so, too much can be made of the racial disparities in job assignments. After all, blacks are also found disproportionately in clerical work and medical specialties with a white-collar orientation, while whites are turning up disproportionately in the blue-collar world of the combat soldier. Likewise, differences within the Army by MOS are neutralized by many common features: the same pay by rank, the same uniform, the same code of discipline, and (not to be overlooked) the same name—"soldier."

Giving of life is the ultimate sacrifice that a soldier can make. That is why the racial composition of the combat arms has been such a contentious issue. Here, black participation has been declining. From 1980 to 1994, the proportion of blacks in the combat arms has fallen from 32 to 24 percent. In other words, relative to their numbers in the U.S. Army, blacks have gone from being slightly overrepresented in the combat arms to being slightly underrepresented. Thus, despite popular perceptions, black males in the Army are not targeted into combat units. It is still true, however, that the proportion of blacks to whites serving in Army combat arms is about twice as high as the proportion of blacks to whites in the American population.

Whatever their military assignments, black soldiers do much better than white solders in one important respect: making it through the initial enlistment. Since the mid-1980s about one white soldier in four has been discharged prematurely for undisciplined behavior, lack of aptitude, physical or psychological problems, and the like. The figure for black male soldiers is one in six. Even among soldiers of similar educational background, blacks are more likely than whites to complete their enlistments. Overall, black soldiers are about one and a half times more likely than whites to complete their enlistments successfully.

Another difference by race cannot be ignored. Black soldiers are almost one and a half times more likely to be incarcerated than white soldiers. (In the other military services the incarceration ratio is two to one.) We cannot say whether this disparity reflects racism in the military justice system, accurately represents criminal activity by race, or both. What we can say is that in civilian prisons, the incarceration ratio of blacks to whites is six to one.[3]

Race relations among enlisted personnel contrast favorably with those in civilian society, but racial harmony does not always prevail. The views of Specialist William Jones (not his real name), a tank mechanic in Germany, are fairly typical of what one hears from junior black enlisted men. Jones, who comes from the Cabrini-Green housing project in Chicago, credits the Army with "having pulled me up, and saving me from the street." He does not mind fixing tanks, but knows that his Army training will not have a direct civilian payoff. Jones regularly sends money home to his mother and also puts $50 a month into an educational fund (the Army matches it twofold). Jones likes the Army but knows it is not perfect.

"You can still bump into an invisible shield of racism, but you have to ignore it," Jones says. "I was at the EM [enlisted members] club and heard a white call someone a nigger the other night. I was shocked to hear it. But I know that we've got to get along together in peacetime if we're going to fight together in wartime." Jones says that when he goes back home, he has little in common with his friends who stayed behind. "They're either locked up or still hanging around waiting for something to happen. They never grow up. They'll always be losers. We don't have much to talk about anymore."

As elsewhere in society, the closest friendships in the Army normally develop between people of similar educational or social backgrounds. In a common pattern on posts large enough to have more than one enlisted club, one of the clubs would become monopolized by one race or the other.

Some soldiers said this reflected different tastes in music more than race per se, but since the mid-1980s, racial integration at enlisted clubs has become much more noticeable. How much of this can be attributed to racial tolerance and how much to the growing crossover appeal of black music to white soldiers cannot be stated with precision.

The high proportion of blacks among male soldiers is exceeded by the even higher proportion of blacks among female soldiers. Blacks now make up about half of all enlisted women (who account for 13 percent of the enlisted ranks overall). Indeed, blacks are now a plurality among Army women: 48 percent compared with 42 percent white and 10 percent other groups. The low attrition rates of black men in the Army is even more pronounced for black women. Afro-American females are twice as likely as white females to complete their enlistments.

The low attrition rates among black women in the Army are not explained easily. Many black women claim that they have more street savvy than their white sisters, are simply better able to meet the physical demands of Army life, or have a better sense of knowing when to "get over" (as gold-bricking is called now) and when not to. Perhaps the main reason blacks, female or male, make a go of it in the Army is simply that for them the grass is not greener in civilian life.

We must not shy away from the sexual dynamics of racial integration. Over the years, black males have been much more likely to date white females than the other way around. At a predominantly black enlisted club, the few whites present are usually female. Few black women are present at the white club. This pattern causes some upset among black women soldiers, who view white women as receiving preferential treatment from black men. In recent years, however, there has been a discernible increase in white male–black female couples, but this is still the exception to the rule in interracial dating.

On the question of intragender relations across races, our survey data are inconclusive. Black soldiers are more likely to say that race relations are better among the women than among the men. White soldiers, on the other hand, say race relations are better among the men than among the women. One generalization does seem warranted. Women apparently are more likely to say that race relations among women are better when the number of women in the unit is small. When females make up a significant number, racial divisions occur among the women. That is, gender overrides race until a critical mass of women—say, 10 percent or more—is present. Then, it seems, race trumps gender.

Perhaps the most striking effect of integration over the past two decades is that enlisted life has become somewhat Afro-Americanized. White soldiers become attuned to Afro-American cultural patterns as fully as black soldiers adapt to "white" culture, if not more so.[4] White junior enlisted soldiers have moved away from a longstanding preference for country-and-western music (although this genre retains a strong following among white NCOs and officers) and now tend to favor rock-and-roll and heavy metal. Disco, soul, reggae, and especially rap, however, also have strong followings among younger white soldiers. Similar, if less pronounced, trends have been noted in civilian culture as well. Clearly, the crossover trend is for whites to acquire Afro-American tastes rather than the other way around. As a white soldier succinctly told us, "In the Army, it's cool to be black."

Perhaps the most vivid example of the "blackening" of enlisted culture is seen in religion. Black Pentecostal congregations have been established on many bases; their services not only attract some whites but have also begun to influence the style of worship in mainstream Protestant services in post chapels.

In March 1993 we attended a service in the Army compound in Mogadishu. Several hundred soldiers were in attendance. The thirty-member choir was almost all black. (The choir's nightly rehearsals added both a religious and a melodious tone to the evenings in the compound.) Halfway through the service, we realized we were watching a black Protestant service, even though the officiating minister and a majority of the congregation were white. Not only was the choir black, but the tone of responses between congregation and minister were also. "Eleven o'clock on Sunday morning is the most segregated hour in America" is a commonplace remark—but not in the Army. Sunday worship in the Army finds both the congregation and the spirit of the service racially integrated.

Sergeants

If the Army has a black center, it is its 75,000 black NCOs. Because blacks are about 50 percent more likely than whites to reenlist after their first hitch, the black presence in the Army is very strong in the senior NCO corps. About a third of first sergeants and sergeants major—company and battalion leaders—are black.

The promotion process to NCO ranks gives us the context for the high status of Afro-Americans in the Army. Soldiers start out as recruits (E–1). During the first enlistment, a soldier can expect to achieve the rank of specialist or corporal (E–4), or, more rarely, sergeant (E–5). Advancement to senior NCO grades—staff sergeant (E–6) and above—takes much longer. A complex formula—weighing test scores, evaluations by superiors, schooling, service records, and interviews with a promotion board—determines who will fill the openings. In twenty years of service, a soldier almost surely will attain the rank of staff sergeant, and most likely will make sergeant first class (E–7). Only exceptional individuals, almost all of whom make the Army a thirty-year career, make master sergeant or first sergeant (E–8), and sergeant major (E–9).

At the very top is the sergeant major of the Army. In 1995 Gene C. McKinney became the first black to attain that rank. Sergeant Major McKinney has four brothers, all of whom served in the Army: Chris served as an officer, Henry retired as a master sergeant, James reached the rank of command sergeant major of the U.S. Army in Europe, and Wilbur served a term in Vietnam.

Most black NCOs profess a kind of bootstrap conservatism. A comparison of black NCO and black civilian responses to a standard survey item is informative. Questions dealt with views on personal responsibility as the main cause of poverty in America. In a national sample, 36 percent of blacks attribute poverty to poor people's lack of trying hard enough, compared to 64 percent of black NCOs (a higher figure, incidentally, than the white national sample).[5] Black NCOs see themselves as the main transmitters of the values of discipline and self-improvement of the old black bourgeoisie. As one senior sergeant stated, "We are the only good role models continuously in contact with young blacks. We have the responsibility of talking values to a captive audience. To keep an eye open only for racism hurts you if you lose sight of the opportunities. Just move ahead."

A first sergeant of a unit at Fort Hood, Texas, who had joined the Army in 1964, put it this way:

> The longer you stay in, the more you can see that racism knows how to hide itself. Still, I owe the Army a lot. When I came in, it was my last option. I wasn't middle class and I sure wasn't upper class. I wasn't even working class. So you know what that leaves. The Army was my only chance to turn myself around, and I took it. I went to Vietnam twice. Along the way I picked up a bachelor's degree, and I'm halfway through my master's. Why did I stay in so long? I wanted to teach young black

soldiers how to make it in a white man's world. If you expect to give orders, you have to learn to take orders. The Army is not going to change for you. It's as simple as that.

Black NCOs easily recognize a part of themselves in the character of Master Sergeant Waters in Charles Fuller's *A Soldier's Play*, which won the 1982 Pulitzer Prize for drama and was made into the film *A Soldier's Story*.[6] Set in the days of the segregated Army, the drama depicts Sergeant Waters as obsessively concerned that blacks not play the fool in front of whites. He can be seen as a martinet or as someone who challenges black soldiers to do their best. The big difference today is that black NCOs lead soldiers of all races.

Black sergeants are offended at any hint that they are partial to blacks. This viewpoint is buttressed by the doctoral dissertation of Charles Hines—probably the only sociologist ever to attain the rank of major general—who, after retiring from the Army, assumed the presidency of Prairie View A&M University in Texas.[7] Hines examined efficiency reports in the early 1980s and found that black sergeants graded "average" black soldiers more severely than did white sergeants. Survey data that we have collected in the 1990s show that black junior enlisted soldiers believe this is still the case. If any racial favoritism is present in superior-subordinate relations, it certainly is not blacks favoring blacks. Afro-American sergeants have a gone long way to assuage whites' feelings of reverse discrimination.

We mentioned Charles Hines's findings to a senior black NCO on a quiet night in the Saudi desert during Desert Shield. The NCO offered this view:

> You have to be harsher with blacks because they say you are a brother and try to play games with you. You can't beat the racism drum forever. You can always find racism. The job is to get on with it. When I see the kid

from the inner city with an attitude, I tell him I'm where I am because I know what's acceptable behavior and what isn't. You know it too.

One black drill sergeant took exception to Hines's findings. His response was succinct: "Whites and blacks equally hate me, or I'm a failure."

Conversely, black sergeants act as mentors and role models for white soldiers as well as black. Of course, white sergeants can do the same for black soldiers, but what makes the Army's enlisted ranks unique is that blacks are more likely to be superiors and whites subordinates. Moreover, the beneficial impact of black sergeants extends beyond the Army. Every year since the late 1970s, some 2,000 black NCOs in the Army (4,000 in the military as a whole) retire from service. This trend will continue into the foreseeable future. Most of these NCOs will be relatively young and looking forward to second careers. The impact of this group of men—and now women as well—on the civilian black community will be tangible and positive.

Officers

In the officer corps in today's Army, one person in nine is black. If officers are the executives of the armed forces, the armed forces boast more black executives than any other institution in the country. The Army's 8,000 black officers come from several places. The most prestigious source of a commission is still the U.S. Military Academy at West Point; about 7 percent of its recent graduating classes have been black. Most officers, however, white or black, come not from West Point but from campus-based detachments of ROTC. These civilian campus-commissioning programs produce six times more officers than the Military Academy. During times of rapid buildup, many officers come up through Officer Candidate School (OCS), a program that has been relatively small since the end of the Vietnam War.

The growth of the black officer corps since 1970 is due largely to the expansion of ROTC at historically black colleges and universities (HBCUs)—the Pentagon's response to the abolition of ROTC at many predominantly white institutions during the Vietnam War. Twenty-one HBCUs, located in the South and border states, today turn out about half of all black Army ROTC commissions. If more ROTC units are more moved from predominantly white institutions in the wake of the controversy about the exclusion of open gays in the military, the proportion of newly commissioned officers from HBCUs will probably increase. The campus culture at any HBCU is unlikely to promote a similar movement to remove ROTC, for few black people would sacrifice an advancement opportunity for young blacks in order to take up the cause of a group they see as consisting primarily of whites who bring discrimination upon themselves by choosing to be open about their sexual orientation.[8] In any event, the significance of the HBCUs in training black leaders for American society must not be overlooked, especially at a time when elite white colleges and universities are making extraordinary efforts to recruit highly qualified black students.

Whether race enters into the officer promotion process remains a point of contention in the military. Equal opportunity assessments conducted in the 1980s showed that black and white officers were selected at about the same rates for the advanced service, war college, and command assignments so important for career advancement. Even so, white officers often believe that blacks are favored in promotion decisions; black officers, in turn, contend that they have to be better qualified than whites in order to advance.

In 1995 it was brought to our attention several times that no black commanded an Army division. This situation is disturbing in that the most senior positions in the Army—three- and four-star billets—usually are filled by candidates from division command.

A very senior black officer gave this blunt appraisal, seconded by most older black officers: "You don't have to be supernigger anymore, but you still have to be better than the rest to make it." Another senior black officer said, "We can run the race with handicaps, but don't expect blacks to perform miracles." He continued, "I'm worried about some of the younger guys. They don't understand that a black still has to do more than a white to get promoted—maybe not as much as before, but still more. If they think equal effort will get equal reward, they've got a big surprise coming."

At the pinnacle of the military hierarchy are the generals. In 1995 there were 24 black generals out of 328 total in the active Army. Eleven more black generals served in the Army Reserve or the National Guard. Some 150 blacks have achieved flag rank in the U.S. military. There have been five four-star generals, Roscoe J. Robinson, Jr., and Johnnie E. Wilson of the Army, Daniel ("Chappie") James and Bernard T. Randolph of the Air Force, as well as Colin L. Powell. Twelve blacks have attained three-star rank. Three black women, all in the Army, have become brigadier generals: Hazel W. Johnson-Brown, Sheria G. Cadoria, and Clara L. Adams-Ender. The promotion of a black to flag rank today is the occasion for little comment.

From our numerous discussions with black generals over the years, it is obvious that they have had extremely satisfying careers. They are rarely shy about their accomplishments or bashful about their patriotism. If they feel any disappointment, it is with their lives after leaving the military. Black generals feel that few of their group attain post-retirement positions commensurate with their abilities. One retiree put it simply, "I will state categorically that few black generals ever get a decent job in the private sector."

This is particularly puzzling, considering that most of these retired black generals once had responsibility for thousands of soldiers and oversaw logistic systems of enormous cost and complexity. Many are familiar with contracting and procurement procedures. Yet consultancies and seats in the boardrooms of the military-industrial complex continue to elude even the most highly qualified black generals. Why? It is difficult not to conclude that the discrimination these people overcame in the military overtakes them again when they return to civilian life.

Senior black leaders in the Army feel a special concern for junior black officers. In 1974 a group of black senior officers founded Rocks, an association named after Brigadier General Roscoe O. Cartwright, who had been killed in an airplane crash the previous year. At the time of his death, Cartwright, or "Rock," as he was better known, was an esteemed role model and mentor for many of the black officers who entered the Army in the 1960s. In 1995 Rocks had a membership of about a thousand black Army officers. Its activities include fund-raising for ROTC scholarships and offering speakers for HBCUs.

The principal mission of Rocks is the same as it has always been—mentoring junior black officers. (An earlier, looser group of black mentors in the Army was known as the Blue Geese.) A retired major general explained, "We want to tell the younger black officers that there will be plenty of bumps on the road, but you have to get over them so you can remove them later for those behind you." This does not mean that Rocks is free of tensions. When senior black officers continually advise junior officers to "be better" or "extra good," many of the younger officers take such advice as ratifying an "unfair" system.

Describing Rocks in the late 1960s, General Powell observed that most of the members

> had peaked professionally, lacking the breaks early on that I was getting. Still, they wanted to help young black officers up the career ladder, give them the inside dope on assignments good and bad, tell them about commanders able or incompetent, and talk up promising candidates to the right people. . . . The spirit of Rocks appealed to me. They looked out for me along the way, and, in turn, I have tried to spot young black military talent and help these officers realize their potential.[9]

The bottom line is that Rocks does not view itself as a pressure group within the Army. Instead, it goes directly to the black community to increase the pool of Afro-American junior officers. Once these junior officers are in the Army, Rocks offers them support and guidance so that they can work and advance within the military system. Here, too, the Army model of black leadership has relevance for the larger society.

4

Handling Contentious Issues

How does the military deal with the tension and outright hostility that too often arise when the races are brought together in America? Consider the case of a drunken white airman whose utterance of a racial slur led to a military appeals court precedent in 1992. The defendant, identified in court papers as Airman Shropshire, who was apprehended and manacled by military policemen for drunk and disorderly conduct, called one of the MPs, a black, "nigger." The airman's conviction under Article 117 of the Uniform Code of Military Justice (UCMJ), which prohibits "provoking speech or gestures," was reversed by a higher military court. The court held that because the police are trained to deal with abusive persons and because Shropshire was handcuffed, there was no reasonable likelihood that the racial epithet would induce a breach of the peace.[1]

In short, the military code seeks only to limit utterances likely to undermine order and discipline, not to deal with statements that hurt feelings or stoke outrage. Regulations narrowly drawn to regulate disruptive conduct—not its symbolic content—have credibility and authority not usually enjoyed by promulgators of university anti-hate codes, for example. At the same time, since the Army does not assume responsibility for protecting Afro-Americans from all racial slights and hard feelings, its codes presume that black soldiers possess an implicit fortitude and self-control.

Perhaps surprisingly, no Army regulation deals solely with race relations or equal opportunity. Instead, these issues fall under Army Regulation (AR) 600–20, whose broad concern is "Army Command Policy." This title is more than symbolic. The Army treats good race relations as a means to readiness and combat effectiveness—not as an end in itself. This is the foundation for the Army's way of overcoming race. Racial concerns are broadened into a general leadership responsibility, and commanders are held accountable for race relations on their watch.

AR 600–20 does not prohibit soldiers from joining racial supremacist groups as long as their activities are "passive"— defined as mere membership or receiving literature in the mail. Army regulations do, however, flatly prohibit soldiers' "participation" in extremist organizations. Prohibited activities include attending meetings or rallies, participating in fund-raising activities, and distributing literature on or off military installations. Any soldier identified as belonging to such a group, even if only as a passive member, will be counseled, however, on the incompatibility of membership with military service. He or she will be reminded that such membership will be considered in overall performance evaluations. In plain language, no further promotions will be forthcoming. Since the Army has essentially an "up or out" system, no promotion means a career cut short.

Some white racist soldiers can fall between the cracks and do attain rank. According to press accounts, Timothy J. McVeigh, the alleged bomber of the federal building in Oklahoma City in April 1995, was reported to have made racist remarks while serving as a sergeant in the U.S. Army. Although the evidence is not conclusive, McVeigh and his cohorts, Michael Fortier and Terry L. Nichols, friends since their Army days, may have drifted in the direction of white supremacist groups after leaving the Army. Whatever the sequence of events, the groups they joined harbored a deep hatred of the federal government and membership would have been an impediment to their careers under Army regulations.

In the aftermath of the 1995 shooting of two black civilians in Fayetteville, North Carolina, by soldiers who belonged to white supremacist organizations, the military's distinction between active and passive membership may disappear. It has yet to be determined (at this writing) whether simple membership in an extremist organization will suffice for expulsion from the armed forces, though it is likely that even passive membership in supremacist organizations will become more circumscribed than it has been.

Contentious racial issues are not always resolved easily. But the Army's approach to equal opportunity, racial complaints, hate speech, and affirmative action points to ways that might make for better race relations in America at large.

Fostering Racial Tolerance

The workhorse of the Army's racial policies is the equal opportunity adviser (EOA). In every command at brigade level or higher, a full-time EOA is responsible for monitoring racial incidents, looking at patterns of race in assignments and promotions, and generally attending to interracial awareness through events like commemorations of Black History Month. Full-time EOAs also train battalion and company NCOs who are assigned equal opportunity responsibilities in addition to their main duties. EOAs, whether full- or part-time, are supposed to be the commander's eyes and ears for the racial climate in the unit.

To emphasize that race relations are everyone's responsibility, the Army does not maintain a corps of permanent equal opportunity advisers. Instead, NCOs from other military specialties rotate through two-year stints in the role before returning to their primary Military Occupational Specialty. This practice assures not only that a large number of NCOs of all races are exposed to assignments that heighten racial sensitivity but also that a permanent corps of EOAs does not develop its own vested interests, with self-serving agendas that might not be conducive to an open racial climate. It also prevents ghettoization of blacks in this field. In 1994 the Army had some 350 full-time EOAs, a ratio of about one to every 1,500 soldiers. In the past, most EOAs were black; today, about half of all EOAs are white, about a third black, and the rest represent other minorities.

In a typical day, an equal opportunity adviser might attend the first formation in the morning, take part in physical training, and visit one of the companies in the brigade. If new arrivals have come to the brigade, the EOA conducts an orientation session for the soldiers and their families. Days may go by with no racial complaints (sexual harassment is more likely to be reported than a racial incident), but when one does occur, the EOA takes action, trying first to work through the chain of command. If the problem lies within the chain of command, the EOA undertakes an investigation and goes to higher authority, if need be. EOAs also keep a record of every discrimination complaint, whether or not it is followed through.

How does the Army take someone who may have little or no experience in dealing with sensitive racial issues and make him or her a standard-bearer for equal opportunity? This is done through the Defense Equal Opportunity Management Institute or, in the inevitable acronym, DEOMI (pronounced "dee-OH-mee") at Patrick Air Force Base in Florida. This office has a staff of 65 military officers and 35 civilians, and its operating budget is close to $2 million, not including military salaries.

When founded in 1971, the organization was called the Defense Race Relations Institute (DRRI).[2] That name reflected its original purpose: to cope with the racial turbulence then afflicting the military. In a telling sign of the racial climate of that era, DRRI was referred to by some of the local inhabitants as "watermelon university" and "razor-blade tech"—appellations well known to the staff and still not forgotten.

With the increasing number of women in the armed forces, the mission for equal opportunity broadened and led to the DEOMI designation in 1979. Indeed, the most significant difference between DRRI and DEOMI is its shift in emphasis from issues of racial discrimination to gender issues and sexual harassment.

The prime function of DEOMI is to produce equal opportunity advisers for the armed services and to foster equal opportunity training throughout the military. Full-time EOAs are trained in a fifteen-week residential course at the school. Besides race and gender relations, the course of instruction covers leadership skills, proficiency in writing and speaking, social psychology, and military policy. Instruction is geared to the college level. DEOMI training also includes nonresidential courses, a "mobile" team that conducts training on military installations, and special courses for Defense Department civilian supervisors. DEOMI receives frequent requests from civilian organizations for advice on setting up race relations programs.

The emphasis at DEOMI is consistently on the value of equal opportunity for military and organizational effectiveness. Thus, the segment on "Racism" falls under the broader rubric of "Cultural Factors and Unit Cohesion." The overriding lesson objective in the "Racism" segment is to equip students with ways "to combat racism that will assist commanders and staff in conducting assessment and investigations."[3] Specific lesson objectives include identifying the language of prejudice, the types of discrimination, the social problems created by racism, and the adverse personal effects of racism. The same pattern is followed in "Personal and Organizational Dissonance," "Concepts of Culture," "Power and Discrimination," and so on.

Most vivid in the memory of older DEOMI graduates is the "shock treatment"—sensitivity-type sessions—administered to bring them "to grips with their underlying racial attitudes." The sensitivity courses veered toward putting whites on the defensive, although whites were never described as racists simply because they occupy a dominant position in American society. A white NCO who went through the early program remembers it as an "eye-opener":

> I never knew American history had anything but white people playing a prominent role. I resented what they were telling me. My reaction was, "This can't be true." Only over time was I able to realize that blacks and whites together made this country what it is today.

This phase of the DEOMI curriculum has since evolved toward a more self-reflective session with a strong element of role-playing: whites seeing situations from the standpoint of a minority member or minority members taking the viewpoint of whites. A senior black official at DEOMI confided to us:

> There was too much negativity against whites in the DRRI days. But we learned and changed from making whites feel guilty to emphasizing military readiness.

The goal now is to show how we all have a stake in good race relations.

Still, students who resist the DEOMI curriculum will be returned to the home unit with a failure on their records.

At first glance, the DEOMI curriculum seems to take an almost trendy multicultural approach to American minority groups. Study sessions and literature are devoted to Afro-Americans, Asian Americans, Jewish Americans, Native Americans, Arab Americans, and Hispanic Americans. Even white Americans get their separate due as part of the American cultural mosaic.

A closer look at the content of the DEOMI offerings, however, reveals significant departures from conventional instruction on multiculturalism. The portion of the curriculum dealing with multiculturalism in American society also falls under "Cultural Factors and Unit Cohesion." Thus, the tie with the core purpose of the military is made explicit—readiness to fight. Indeed, DEOMI's mission statement reads: "We teach equal opportunity (fairness) is a commander's program and a combat readiness issue." Likewise, in the DEOMI philosophy, subgroups' cultures and expressions must be appreciated without losing sight of the common ground shared by all Americans, what Arthur Schlesinger, Jr., calls our country's "unifying ideals."[4] The DEOMI message is that an overarching, common American identity must override cultural diversity.

The bottom-line question for an equal opportunity adviser is simple: Does it help or handicap a military career? In the 1970s and early 1980s, being a race relations NCO could have easily marginalized a soldier's position in the Army. Virtually all EOAs were, in their own words, "drafted"—involuntarily sent to DEOMI. In recent years, the picture has changed toward the positive.

We have asked equal opportunity advisers in various posts

about their career prospects. Some said that being an EOA was a "good ticket to be punched" on the way up to first sergeant or sergeant major. Yet, as one EOA sergeant told us: "If you get back-to-back EOA assignments you can't get promoted to save your life." Just about all of the EOAs mentioned that a strong plus in DEOMI training was the emphasis on writing and speaking proficiency. This kind of training develops general leadership skills that can only enhance an NCO's career. The consensus appears to be that an EOA assignment will not hurt a career and will probably, but not surely, be an advantage for future promotion.

In 1987 DEOMI branched out from its exclusive training function and began to conduct serious social research. A Directorate of Research was established to conduct social scientific studies on equal opportunity programs. A significant accomplishment was the development of the Military Equal Opportunity Climate Survey (MEOCS) in 1990 by Mickey R. Dansby and Dan Landis.[5] This sophisticated survey instrument is perhaps the most valid, as well as the most reliable, measure of the equal opportunity climate ever created.[6] The MEOCS seeks to measure several basic dimensions. One deals with organizational factors that include commitment to the organization, effectiveness of the mission, and job satisfaction. Another deals more directly with racial factors, including perceptions of discrimination against minorities, "reverse discrimination," and racial separatism. A third dimension deals with gender issues.

An MEOCS can be conducted only at a commander's request. EOAs conduct the actual survey and the professional staff at DEOMI makes the analysis. The findings are given to the commander, who "owns the data." He or she need not show them to anyone. Yet some commanders are reluctant to use MEOCS, for fear that a negative race (or gender) picture will blemish their records. The more confident use MEOCS to determine whether any corrective action should be taken before racial troubles become serious. A revision of AR 600–20 in 1994 recommends that within ninety days of taking command, all new commanders conduct an assessment of the equal opportunity climate in their unit. MEOCS, now used widely throughout the services, is readily applicable in a variety of settings outside the military.

MEOCS surveys furnish information on how various groups judge the racial and gender climate in the military. Over the years, a consistent pattern has appeared:

Responses	Group
Most positive	1. White male officers
	2. White male enlisted
	3. White female officers*
	4. White female enlisted
	5. Minority male officers
	6. Minority male enlisted
	7. Minority female enlisted
Least positive	8. Minority female officers

*Almost the same as 2.

Not surprisingly, individuals in superordinate groups—whites, men, officers—perceive less discrimination than members of subordinate groups—minorities, women, enlisted. The only exceptions to this pattern are minority female officers, who are more negative regarding the equal opportunity climate than minority enlisted women. We suggest that this is so because minority female officers, unlike their enlisted counterparts, have fewer peers and therefore a weaker interpersonal support system. Most noteworthy, however, is that race trumps every other status.

What have DEOMI and the military learned about teaching race relations courses? First, DRRI viewed equal opportunity as primarily the responsibility of a specialized staff; DEOMI regards it as part of a commander's general responsibilities. Also, DRRI often used confrontational teaching techniques; DEOMI views problem-solving as the proper pedagogy in race relations. DRRI sought to change underlying attitudes; DEOMI deals with observable behavior. Most important, DRRI considered equal opportunity an end in itself; DEOMI treats equal opportunity as the means to combat readiness. The DRRI and DEOMI experiences did share one lesson: good social science research is better than intuition for leaders seeking to ascertain and deal with racial problems within their organizations.

At least as important as any changes in the Army's equal opportunity curriculum is the environment in which it is delivered. Unlike the "sensitivity" or multicultural seminars provided in most civilian settings, the Army's race relations courses do not take place in a single-race setting. The Army experience shows that the quality of race relations courses differs dramatically when the black proportion is large, and blacks make up a large percentage of almost any Army audience.

Equal Opportunity Complaints

If a soldier makes a discrimination complaint that is found to be justified, the chain of command must act to improve the racial climate. Even in those cases where a discrimination complaint is not substantiated, the chain of command must still act to improve the racial climate, for AR 600–20 specifies that commanders must take action to "resolve the perception of unfair treatment."[7] That is, commanders are responsible for the general racial climate in their units as well as for handling specific charges of discrimination. A poisoned racial climate is the enemy of any officer who wishes to advance in the Army.

Soldiers who believe that they have suffered discrimination are expected to go first to their immediate commanders. Commanders are obligated to investigate quickly, usually within two weeks. This action can range from informal inquiries with no paperwork to formal investigations that are empowered to take sworn testimony. If a complaint is substantiated, commanders must take appropriate steps, ranging from counseling, to a one-stripe demotion, to administrative action (such as a poor evaluation or a bar to reenlistment), all the way up to formal legal action. Another critical aspect of this process is the policy that soldiers who knowingly make a fraudulent complaint can be punished under the military justice system. The possibility that complainants can be sanctioned undoubtedly reduces the number of complaints, both warranted and unwarranted.

If the offended soldier believes he or she cannot obtain satisfaction from the chain of command, perhaps because the commander himself is the source of the trouble, other recourses are possible. These include going to the inspector general, the chaplain, the Judge Advocate Corps, or, most usually, the equal opportunity adviser. Whatever the case, soldiers who feel they have a grievance related to racial discrimination cannot look to remedies outside the military system. Members of the armed forces cannot use civilian courts to seek redress of individual mistreatment. Courts have upheld this principle on the grounds that allowing grievances to be taken to civilian courts would undermine the discipline necessary to accomplish the military mission.[8]

The vast majority of complaints center on racial slurs and slights, but these can usually be handled informally by the equal opportunity adviser. The difficult complaints revolve around evaluations, promotions, or assignment to special Army schools. In 1994 the Army received 686 formal complaints concerning racial bias, virtually all filed by members of minority groups. Most of these concerned promotions or related issues. About one complaint in five was judged to have cause.

These figures say several things. First, the low absolute number of complaints implies that most are being resolved at the company level by commanders and equal opportunity advisers. Second, the low ratio of substantiated complaints shows that soldiers' perceptions of being discriminated against often cannot be supported with evidence that will stand up in a formal investigation.

Hate Speech

One night in the barracks, a white soldier shouts "nigger" at a black soldier. Several blacks jump the white soldier. A barracks melee breaks out, in which the races go at each other. The next day everybody tensely awaits new trouble. What is to be done? This scenario from the DEOMI curriculum has a prescribed or "school" solution. The NCOs are supposed to let everybody cool off, talk to their soldiers in groups and individually, bring in an officer if necessary, and ascertain exactly what happened. A racial epithet is cause for punishment in the Army if it is an incitement to riot. If the aggrieved party engages in action involving physical assault, he too can be punished. If the epithet is directed against a superior, the soldier can also be charged with disrespect. If the act is committed by a superior, the offender can be charged with conduct unbecoming an NCO or officer.

The scenario of the racial epithet brings us to the Army's policies toward hate speech. In contrast to the situation under the speech codes that have developed on many university campuses, in the armed forces racial slurs in and of themselves are not an offense. Punishment is invoked only when expressions cause trouble. As with complaints of racial discrimination, the racial content of a "provoking" remark is subsumed into a general consideration of command responsibility.

Hate speech, then, is never a "stand-alone" offense. A racial slur is almost always punished under Article 117—"Provoking Speeches or Gestures"—of the Uniform Code of Military Justice (UCMJ). Under Article 117, words that are "provoking are those which are used in the presence of the person to whom they are directed and which a reasonable person would expect to induce a breach of the peace under the circumstances."[9] The use of provoking words is viewed in connection with other offenses such as assault, disobedience, or upsetting order and discipline. Similarly, characterizing someone's mother in unfavorable terms, for example, is punishable under Article 117 if it causes a breach of the peace.

The basis of Article 117 in American military jurisprudence dates back at least to 1775 to the Articles of War (predecessor of the UCMJ)—and, in some interpretations, back to feudal English law.[10] The relevant article for punishing racial epithets, then, originates in an old military tradition and a time when the concept of hate speech was unknown.

Article 117 specifically excludes from "provoking words" reprimands that may "properly be administered in the interest of training, efficiency, or discipline in the armed forces." Article 93, which pertains to maltreatment of subordinates, might be invoked in the case of a superior's use of racial epithets toward a subordinate. Article 133, dealing with "Conduct Unbecoming," also might be used to support convictions in which superiors direct epithets toward subordinates. Usually this occurs in training, where drill sergeants are wont to use abusive language toward trainees.

What really happens in the barracks when someone uses an epithet or, more commonly, a racial stereotype? Soldiers frequently use these terms in a teasing manner. One first sergeant explains:

The trouble starts when someone crosses the line. He doesn't know the others as well as he thinks he does. Or someone from outside the group of teasers joins in. You know you're overstepping when someone punches you in the nose. And in the case of two evenly matched fighters, there is a good chance that nothing will be done beyond a slap on the wrist.

Once a fight starts, however, both sides are to be punished. In ascending order of severity, punishment can consist of informal counseling, signing a counseling statement, "extra training" (a longer workday for a specified period), or a formal reprimand. At the middle level is an "Article 15," also known as "company punishment." This can include demotion by one rank, restriction to the area, or a light fine. Company punishment does not become part of a soldier's permanent record. Of course, if a felony is committed in the act of the epithet, court-martial proceedings would be in order.

Unlike anti-hate speech codes in colleges and universities, the criteria in the Army are clearly based on consequential rather than symbolic or expressive grounds. Hate-speech restrictions on college campuses are defended on the grounds that they work against an environment where mutual dialogue must be preserved. In the Army, hate speech incurs sanctions only when it upsets order and discipline or provokes a breach of the peace. Also, unlike the situation in civilian hate crimes, the culprit's motive is not a factor in military law. By contrast, many civilian laws do take motive into account. This approach was validated in a 1992 Supreme Court decision that permits jurisdictions to impose extra punishment for crimes motivated by racial hatred.[11] In short, the military focuses on behavior, not on the remarks themselves.

In another contrast between the Army post and the college campus, soldiers are more likely to feel that bad race relations reflect directly on their unit's reputation. Students do not share this perception. Instead, they feel that their behavior does not have an influence on the perception of their university. Whereas college students often seek public redress and attention regarding racial incidents on college campuses, both black and white soldiers often seek to downplay racial slights. The Army bombards soldiers with the message that racial divisiveness ruins cohesion, which in turn results in unnecessary deaths in war. Even in peacetime, such divisiveness makes any mission all the more difficult to accomplish.

The Army's relative tolerance of hate speech must be understood in light of the strong black presence in leadership positions. The Army works because blacks trust this system much more than their civilian counterparts do theirs. The significance of having many black superiors and white subordinates to develop such organizational trust can scarcely be overstated. Henry Louis Gates, Jr., of Harvard University, makes the profound point that hate speech is more incendiary when the targeted group has occupied a historical and contemporary position of subordination.[12] In the Army, where blacks are well represented in positions of authority, the expectation that blacks must sometimes tolerate hurtful words is not as unreasonable as it might seem at first glance.

Affirmative Action, Goals, and Quotas

The guidelines for Army promotion boards state: "The goal for this board is to achieve a percentage of minority and female selection not less than the selection rate for all officers being considered." The pressure to meet the goal is strong, and the goal is met in most cases. If the goal is not met, however, and if further review indicates that it cannot be met without violating standards, then the chips fall where they may. Significantly, the goals are not linked to any timetables.

The promotion process goes like this. The board takes into consideration past assignments, physical standards, evaluation ratings, education, and promotability to the next level above the one under consideration. The strongest candidates are promoted quickly; the weakest are eliminated quickly. In reality, the goals become operative only in the gray middle. As one well-informed white officer said, "Only fully qualified people are promoted, but not necessarily the best qualified. But don't forget we are talking micromillimeter differences in these cases."

If this system looks like a quota by another name, take another look. A 1995 study by the General Accounting Office (GAO) found that Army promotions for minorities to midlevel officer positions lagged behind that of whites.[13] The number of blacks who are promoted from captain to major and from major to lieutenant colonel—virtual prerequisites for an officer seeking an Army career—usually falls short of the goal. Disparities in promotion by race are not in and of themselves indications of racial discrimination, however. Such disparities might alternatively be viewed as a sign that standards are not being compromised, and redound to the long-term advantage of those who are promoted. It is when equally (or better) qualified blacks are less likely to receive promotions that we can assert that racism, overt or covert, causes the disparities. Significantly, the GAO study found no racial discrepancies for promotions at the most senior levels. Indeed, at the general officer level, blacks are promoted slightly in excess of their numbers in the pool.

The lag in the promotion of black captains and majors, nevertheless, causes the Army command heartburn, and creates frustration among black officers. The most plausible explanation for the shortfall is that a disproportionate number of black junior officers have not acquired the writing and communication skills necessary for promotion to staff jobs. (Efforts to overcome these deficiencies are described in the next chapter.) Even so, in 1994, two white male former officers were preparing a class-action lawsuit against the Army for what they called reverse discrimination in the promotion system.[14] According to a senior Army lawyer in the Judge Advocate's office, if the plaintiffs could demonstrate that a promotion board set a quota for promotion by race, the Army could be sued; this officer observed further that the current policy of goals without timetables is "walking pretty close to the edge."

We must stress that the goals in the Army promotion process are based not on the number of minority members in the Army, but on the number of minority members in the pool of potential promotees to the next higher rank. This criterion cuts through much of the thicket surrounding affirmative action in civilian life and allows for some picking and choosing among numerous minority candidates. Beyond the numbers implied in goals, however, must be a longer range aim: placing blacks in junior positions that serve as launching pads for future promotions. In the Army, this entails some command time away from staff positions. In simple terms, enough blacks must be present in the promotion pool to make affirmative action work well.

For a better idea of how these policies work in practice, consider how they might apply in the academic world. In that case, hiring committees would strive to hire a number of minority new assistant professors roughly equal to the minority proportion of recent Ph.D.'s in a given field; the proportionate number of associate professors should approximate the number of assistant professors; the number of full professors should aim for the same percentage as found among associate professors. (Point of information: blacks accounted for 3.1 percent of all Ph.D.'s awarded in 1993; excluding doctorates in education, 2.1 percent of all

Ph.D.'s.)[15] The impact of such a policy is to focus long-term equal opportunity efforts on expanding the number of minority candidates entering the pipeline, rather than struggling to fill a specified number of slots from a disproportionately small number of qualified candidates.

Establishing and maintaining standards may cause short-term turmoil, as it did in the Army of the 1970s, but it also means that individuals who attain senior positions are fully qualified. In poor affirmative action, an organization promotes less qualified people to buy temporary peace but invites long-term disaffection. The Army was able to accomplish its goal partly because it contained no purportedly liberal constituency willing to accept an initial drop in standards.

Blacks who were promoted in the early days had a self-confidence that made them the strongest defenders of standards for their own black subordinates. Among people who understand the Army's promotion policies, blacks promoted to positions of authority bear no stigma. No identifiable group of underqualified minority members occupies leadership positions in the Army.

By resisting political pressure to adopt quotas in the early stages of its affirmative action, the Army limited trouble for itself and for the beneficiaries of affirmative action in later years. A retired black general reminisced:

> We lost a lot of fine black junior officers who were just as good as the whites who were promoted. Or at least close enough because there's always some subjectivity involved. But by their paying the penalty, it meant that those of us who made it were never looked upon as beneficiaries of racial favoritism.

The military does not elaborately disguise its goals or its methods for attaining them because it does not have to deal with the fundamental fact that drives quota systems in civilian institutions: the dearth of qualified blacks.[16] In contrast with admissions at certain universities, the military has no hint of two promotion lists in which whites are compared only with whites, blacks only with blacks. Among 301 universities across the country, only 34 percent of black students who enrolled as freshmen in 1984–87 graduated within six years. For whites, the overall graduation rate was 57 percent, nearly double the rate for blacks.[17] In the Army, by way of contrast, blacks are more likely than white soldiers to complete their enlistments.

An emphasis on standards can work only if it goes hand in hand with a true commitment to equal opportunity, and vice versa. As the sociologist Seymour Martin Lipset points out, most Americans make a critical distinction between compensatory action and preferential treatment.[18] Compensatory action helps members of disadvantaged groups to meet the standards of competition. In preferential treatment, those standards are suspended: quotas are adopted to favor persons on the basis of their membership in groups instead of on merit. Most Americans support compensatory action, but majorities of both blacks and whites consistently oppose quotas.

On the sticky issue of racial representation in promotions, the Army has come up with a system that satisfies neither the pro-quota nor the anti-quota viewpoints—but it works. Although affirmative action in the Army does have its tensions, it is not a prescription for loss of self-esteem by blacks or resentment by whites.

Fundamental to the Army's approach is forthright acknowledgment of the significance of race in personnel decisions. On the most basic level, a smart platoon sergeant makes sure that no squad consists of soldiers all of one color. As a result, people are moved around deliberately with regard to race. White battalion and company commanders seek out black sergeants major or first sergeants, and vice versa. Indeed, we would be surprised to learn of the existence of a black company commander in the Army with a black first sergeant. Is this interference with a race-blind selection process? Of course it is. But so be it. The results speak for themselves.

Race-Savvy, Not Race-Blind

The Army is not race-blind; it is race-savvy. Cognizance of race is used to further nonracist goals. The resulting policies show both the limits and the potentialities of social engineering to improve race relations. Mandatory courses in race relations are not magic bullets, but they send a strong signal to black soldiers that the Army is serious about equal opportunity. Recognition of multiculturalism and ethnic diversity is subordinated to the Army's overriding goal of combat readiness. Almost every official way of addressing race is premised on the idea that the Army works best when race relations are harmonious and racial justice is upheld. This is the most effective way of convincing white and black soldiers that they have to get along. Making equal opportunity a general leadership responsibility further emphasizes the unifying structure and culture of the military organization.

Another lesson must be mentioned. During its racial troubles in the 1970s, the Army developed and conducted the most extensive research program on equal opportunity in history. The Army Research Institute for the Behavioral and Social Sciences (ARI) funded extensive analyses of race relations, unequaled by any civilian research agency.[19] The role of black social scientists was pivotal in this project. Research by James A. Thomas and Peter Nordlie found that the Army's initial courses in race relations were producing white backlash sentiments. Richard O. Hope, then director of research at DRRI, conducted extensive evaluation studies that led to the mainstreaming of race relations programs into the command structure. John Sibley Butler statistically isolated the effect of institutional racism on enlisted promotion rates and showed that "smarter" blacks were less likely to be promoted than blacks with lower test scores.[20] This finding was the most damning evidence of racism in Army promotion procedures. The contemporary surveys on racial climate developed by ARI and DEOMI continue an impressive research tradition.

Most important, perhaps, is the fact that the Army does not patronize or infantilize blacks by implying that they need special standards in order to succeed or that they must be treated with kid gloves at all times. At the same time, the basically equal position of the races reduces blacks' tendency to be exceptionally sensitive to every possible racial slight or to view malignant racism as an explanation for everything bad that happens to them in the Army. This situation suggests that the real aim of those seeking to improve race relations is not to emphasize racial preferences or multicultural indoctrination. Instead, members of a historically disadvantaged population should be given the tools they need to compete with the more privileged.

Fulfillment of this goal requires a significant commitment of resources for compensatory efforts; this commitment has been made by the Army, though not yet by American society. A level playing field is not always enough.

5

Preparing Soldiers for a Level Playing Field

Social background will never again be as inconsequential in a soldier's Army career as during basic training. The physical rigors of infantry training, the uniform, the mandatory short haircuts, to name just a few features of recruit life, all reduce preexisting civilian distinctions. Indeed, one of the conventional explanations for black achievement in the Army is that black and white recruits start their military life on a level playing field.

Alas, the "level playing field" characterization of the Army is sometimes taken too far. The more closely we look at blacks' achievement in the Army, the harder it becomes to dismiss the consequences of prior social status.

Even before enlistment, young people face numerous obstacles to a successful Army career. If they are deficient in basic skills, they cannot enlist in the first place. Many young blacks are barred from service because they fail to meet minimum entrance requirements, especially in achievement test scores. After enlistment, opportunities for promotion to the NCO levels are correlated with educational attainment and scores on proficiency tests—formidable hurdles for anyone who has not had access to quality education. Further up the hierarchy, the officer corps effectively excludes all persons without a college degree. Finally, within the officer ranks, promotions depend heavily on advanced writing and communication skills. For all these reasons, some form of compensatory action is often needed before soldiers can truly be said to play on the proverbial level field.

The Army does not lower its standards; it elevates its recruits and soldiers. This is one of the most important characteristics of the Army's approach to matters of race, one well worth transferring to the civilian world. Flowing from this approach is one of the Army's most significant lessons for race relations: disadvantaged youths can be made to meet demanding standards. Four programs are devoted to doing precisely that.

One program brings young people up to enlistment standards, while another raises enlisted soldiers to NCO standards. A third brings black undergraduates to officer-commissioning standards, and a fourth raises high school graduates to West Point–admission standards. Each program is worthy of a book in its own right. That no such books have been written shows how little attention the civilian world has paid to the achievement of blacks within the armed forces.

Raising Recruits to Enlistment Standards

In the late 1980s, Jane S. Borne was distressed to learn that half of the young men and women from Mississippi who wanted to enlist in the military could not do so because of mathematics and reading deficiencies. Though particularly severe in Mississippi, the problem was hardly unique to that state. During the 1980s and early 1990s, about a third of all black youths and a quarter of whites in the United States were ineligible for service, mainly because of low scores on the Armed Services Vocational Aptitude Battery (ASVAB), the military's entrance test.[1] Borne, a native Mississippian who in the early 1970s had been the first white teacher in an all-black elementary school in North Gulfport, Mississippi, decided to take action. With the help of a colleague, Gail Clark Cotton, she formed an innovative pilot program designed to recruit young people who had failed the ASVAB and to give them a second chance.

Borne and Cotton presented their idea to Gerald Turner, chancellor of the University of Mississippi. Persuaded by the merits of the proposal, Turner offered the facilities at Gulf Coast Community College, in Perkinston, for the project. In April 1990 the Pre-Military Development Program (PMDP) opened its doors, funded by the state of Mississippi and the federal Job Training Partnership Act. The state and federal funds were augmented by a Department of Defense grant, made possible through the efforts of Congressman Sonny Montgomery (D-Miss.) and W. Steve Sellman, director of accessions for the Department of Defense.

From the beginning, Borne and Cotton viewed the project as a national model for creating opportunities for disadvantaged youths to join the armed forces. Over its two-year life, the PMDP enrolled a total of 296 students, in groups of about 30 students at a time. All the students had failed the ASVAB, but each had been recommended for the program by recruiting sergeants who thought the applicant had a chance of passing the test at a second opportunity. The program was in great demand; there were always more applicants than places.

Entrants into the program had only one goal: to pass the ASVAB with a score high enough to gain entrance into the military. No definite time was set for the length of the course. Students took three weeks to five months to pass the course; the average stay was about six weeks.

The students received free tuition and living arrangements. They were assigned dormitory rooms on the Gulf Coast campus and could eat three meals a day in the college cafeteria. Counseling and academic services were provided at no charge. On weekends the students could go home or stay on campus.

The Pre-Military Development Program relied heavily on a self-paced computer instruction system. A donation by the Control Data Corporation of the CYBER-Based Instructional System (CYBIS) made this possible.[2] CYBIS includes 10,000 hours of computer lessons. The lessons are repeated in different forms until the student understands the material. Each PMDP student had to cover a hundred hours of CYBIS to upgrade weak skills in mathematics and English.

The core part of the PMDP pedagogy was reading, writing, and mathematics. The schedule was heavily regimented and also included two and a half hours of physical training. A typical daily schedule began with breakfast at 7 A.M. and ended with lights out at 11 P.M. During the day three and a half hours were devoted to CYBIS or classes, two hours to life-coping skills, and two hours to self-paced study on a computer.

What was the upshot? Eighty-eight percent of the students increased two to three grade levels in reading comprehension and mathematics, all in about six weeks. Among those for whom full information is available, 46 percent passed the ASVAB upon retaking it, 33 percent changed their minds about enlisting in the military and instead found civilian employment or enrolled in a school or college, and 11 percent were waiting to retake the ASVAB when the program was terminated. Only 10 percent dropped out of the program. Because the Gulf Coast program had no resources for a follow-up study of all participants, the eventual outcomes for 30 percent are unknown.

The PMDP had a built-in mechanism to screen out people who were unlikely ever to pass the ASVAB. Each student had been recommended by recruiting sergeants, who presumably would not have backed students who presented no hope of eventual admission into the armed forces. Still, the enrollees were clearly from Mississippi's disadvantaged class: 71 percent were black, mainly from rural areas; about 20 percent were female. Few of the students had had contact with their fathers.

Borne and Cotton offer the following reflections on what occurred beyond quantifiable findings. Because CYBIS software avoids cartoons and is not in color, the students perceived it as serious material for adults, not a video game for teenagers. Borne and Cotton also learned something unexpected about literacy skills: writing could be improved greatly by encouraging poetry composition. Many students found paragraphs too intimidating at the beginning, but they took to poetry, once told that the lines need not rhyme.

In addition, the students wanted the program to be much more military. Cotton states, "They would have loved marching and military saluting." Borne agrees, saying, "They certainly wanted to wear uniforms." Borne and Cotton also believe that the women enrollees were noticeably more goal-oriented than the men. Perhaps because of a fear of failure, the young men were likely to show less commitment and would tease fellow students who were doing well. Still, the overriding conclusion for all enrollees was clear: completion of the course meant entrance into the military.

Is the success rate of the Pre-Military Development Program worth the cost? The budget for the Gulf Coast pilot project came to only $2,000 per slot per year, much less than a self-sustaining program would need to operate without donated facilities and computers. Because the facilities and computer instruction system were donated, project funds went only to salaries for five teachers, one counselor, and a small office staff. Borne and Cotton have prepared a proposal for a three-month residential camp on the Gulf Coast model, at a cost of around $4,000 per participant. They would like to test the pedagogical principles that worked in the Gulf Coast program to see whether they will assist low-income urban youth, a higher risk group than the original enrollees.[3] The potential payoff in improved academic strengths among largely poor black youths is tremendous. Yet the Borne and Cotton proposal remains unfunded.

As is apparent by now, we do not advocate lowering standards to accommodate otherwise excluded groups. However, the story of the Army's experience with disadvantaged recruits would not be complete without citing two prominent cases in which the Army did lower barriers to enlistment. One intentional case was Project 100,000, conducted during the Vietnam War; the other was the unintentional acceptance of low-scoring recruits during the early years of the all-volunteer force.[4] Many of the underqualified recruits achieved successes that countered initial expectations. One lesson emerged from these experiences: while standards are important, the Army can and does make soldiers out of less than ideal recruits. Indeed, during manpower shortages, the definition of "ideal" has proved quite malleable.

Beginning in 1966, under the initiative of Secretary of Defense Robert S. McNamara, the Army began drafting

100,000 men a year under "new standards." McNamara framed Project 100,000 as part of the War on Poverty, an opportunity to change the lives of disadvantaged young men. Whether wartime conscripts would have welcomed this kind of assistance is questionable, but the fact is that Project 100,000 quadrupled the number of entrants from the lowest mental aptitude test groups. Blacks accounted for a disproportionate 36 percent of the program's conscripts, while half were high school dropouts.

Project 100,000 drew severe criticism from both military leaders and political liberals. Military leaders regarded the "new standards" entrants as lowering the quality of recruits and expected an increase in disciplinary problems to follow. Liberals viewed these men as cannon fodder, given their socioeconomic backgrounds and their ultimate destination; a disproportionate number were assigned to the combat arms. Unexpectedly, Project 100,000 men did only marginally worse than other recruits in completing their tours, although they received noticeably fewer promotions.[5]

The other experience with poorly qualified recruits occurred in the late 1970s. Due to a miscalibration of ASVAB scores, more than 300,000 lower aptitude men—subsequently known as "potentially ineligibles" (PIs)—were inadvertently accepted into the military. The PIs in heavy-labor occupations were barely distinguishable from other soldiers in completion of tours and had only marginally lower promotion rates, but PIs in military specialties that required reading and technical skills were much more likely to do poorly on all counts.

Follow-up studies showed that Project 100,000 and PI veterans fared no better in terms of income and occupation than a control group of nonveterans. (Still, by a three-to-one margin, the veterans viewed military service as having had a positive rather than a negative effect on their lives.) The disadvantages that accompany low-aptitude levels cannot be rectified solely by a term of military service. The Army can, however, offer forms of remedial and additional education that can dramatically raise achievement levels.

Rising to NCO Standards

At more than 150 Army education centers around the world, nearly 100,000 soldiers are enrolled in some kind of continuing education. In recent years, the trend has been away from tuition grants for off-post education, toward on-post education with free tuition. One such program is Functional Academic Skills Training (FAST). Whereas the Gulf Coast program was devoted to bringing young people into the armed forces, FAST seeks to move lower ranking enlisted people into the noncommissioned officer ranks.

Company commanders never like to lose troops to education programs during duty time. The first such program, the Basic Skills Education Program (BSEP), was inaugurated in 1966 to serve the needs of the Project 100,000 recruits. BSEP provided basic literacy instruction and elementary arithmetic to support military occupational specialty training. But with the rise in enlistment standards in the 1980s, BSEP has become less significant.

BSEP II, inaugurated in 1985, differed from its predecessor in that it was directed toward soldiers with leadership and promotion potential. Formal entry into BSEP II was based on a commander's decision, discussion with the soldier concerned, and consultation with the educational counselor on post. In theory, every soldier's test score should be examined as he comes closer to promotion. In fact, BSEP II was invaluable for enlisted soldiers who needed to raise their entrance test scores in order to qualify for various Army service schools or upgrades in their military occupational specialty, prerequisites for promotion to NCO.

Partly to emphasize that the enrollees in BSEP II were considered promotable and to avoid the "dummy" label that had accompanied the initial Basic Skills Education Program, the Army changed the name of the program to Functional Academic Skills Training (FAST) in 1992. Each student undergoes a diagnostic placement test and signs a "learning contract," specifying the competencies to be mastered and the dates for the retests. The key test is the General Technical or "GT" (e.g., arithmetic reasoning, world knowledge, paragraph comprehension) part of the ASVAB. Optimal instruction is four hours a day in classes ranging in size from 10 to 20 students, and students can participate in the program for up to 180 hours. In reality, although test scores are important in the promotion system, tests can be retaken after enrollment in remedial education in FAST. After a certain time, however, a soldier who cannot raise his or her scores sufficiently is asked to leave the program.

The quality of FAST instructors can vary from post to post and within the same military installation. Staff members interviewed about educational formats said the best results came with a tutor in a learning center with computer facilities. Next best came a tutor without computer instruction, followed by a traditional classroom. Last was the soldier working on his own with self-paced computer, textbooks, or both.

In 1995 the Army was taking steps to computerize the FAST curriculum into forty-one standard lessons. This arrangement would allow a soldier who is transferred from one post to another to resume instruction precisely where he left off. The material covered is related to the skills required of particular occupational groups within the Army, but the content always develops competency in reading, writing, and mathematical skills.

Twenty-three lessons deal with mathematics, eleven with reading, and seven with writing. The mathematics curriculum starts with counting and identifying properties of numbers and proceeds to addition, subtraction, multiplication, and division of whole numbers. Next it advances to conversion of decimals, fractions, and percentages; reconciling a checkbook; and using a military map. The curriculum concludes with algebraic equations, trigonometry, and logarithms. The reading lessons include, in sequence: following directions; defining common English and technical military words; locating information by using tables of contents, indexes, glossaries; organizing information from multiple sources; and obtaining information from diagrams and charts. The writing course begins with spelling common English words and with basic rules of grammar and punctuation. It continues with note-taking and concludes with rewriting paragraphs for clarity. Completion of FAST brings the soldier well into college-level work. Of course, the highest levels of competency are not necessary for most NCO promotions.

The nub of the issue in FAST is how to secure a soldier's release from duty time. Half time for three weeks is the norm, but this arrangement often requires "creative scheduling." As one education counselor put it:

> We must fight the company commanders because they don't want to lose a soldier. But you have to set an atmosphere that this is the best and fairest way to reward a good soldier. "Sergeant So and So has to raise his GT score. If he doesn't, he'll never be promoted." If you phrase it this way, you're more likely to convince the company commander. If you can get the students in the morning, you're really living in heaven.

Instructors in FAST are state-certified teachers in adult education. On small posts, the continuing education office contracts directly with local teachers. On large installations, the contract is made with colleges and for-profit providers of educational services. From a teacher's perspective, the problem is that Army employment in continuing education can be intermittent.

Some 60,000 soldiers, 60 percent of them black, are enrolled in a FAST program at any time. In terms of minority participation, the Army's continuing education program is the largest in existence. Without FAST, the strong black representation in the NCO corps would be impossible.

Raising Black Undergraduates to Officer-Commissioning Standards

There are 117 historically black colleges and universities (HBCUs) in the United States, nearly all in Southern and border states. A few HBCUs predate the Civil War, more were founded during Reconstruction, and still others were established in the decades before and after the turn of the century. These HBCUs have played a prominent role in black America. Indeed, no other institution in this country—black or predominantly white—produces so many black leaders for American society.

Less well known is their value as a major source of black military officers. In 1995, of the 3,963 ROTC commissions, 436 (11 percent) were awarded to Afro-Americans. Almost half this number, 194, went to students at the 28 HBCUs with Army ROTC programs on their campus. The largest programs are at Alabama A&M University, Tuskegee University in Alabama, Florida A&M University, Jackson State University in Mississippi, Howard University in Washington, D.C., North Carolina A&T State University, South Carolina State College, Prairie View A&M University in Texas, and in Virginia, Hampton University and Norfolk State University.

It is fair to say that antimilitary sentiments are typically fashionable among many professors, black and white, at America's major universities. ROTC units at HBCUs, however, enjoy a prestige that would be the envy of units at most predominantly white campuses. Professors of military science at HBCUs are often revered names in the black officers' world. ROTC mentors who are remembered with respect by contemporary black officers include Colonel James Robinson at South Carolina State and Lieutenant Colonel Hiram Chase, who served both at Howard and Prairie View.

A black applicant to an ROTC program is twice as likely as a white applicant to be awarded an ROTC scholarship because a special scholarship allotment—the Quality Enrichment Program—exists for ROTC cadets at HBCUs. By directing such scholarships to HBCUs, the Army's Cadet Command—the ROTC's parent organization—hopes to meet its goal of awarding one-fifth of all new commissions to blacks. The four-year ROTC scholarship pays for tuition, fees, and books, and it provides a $1,000 annual stipend. The lesson here is clear: to produce black leaders, in this case military officers, the pool from which they come, ROTC units, must be increased.

The Army recognizes that some ROTC students in the HBCUs lack the written, verbal, and mathematical skills needed to compete successfully with their contemporaries in military careers. In 1985 this recognition led to Enhanced Skills Training (EST) at HBCUs with ROTC programs. Cadets are evaluated through a writing sample and standardized reading and mathematical tests. Average or below-average scorers must enroll in EST as an additional requirement. Teachers are hired on contract by the Cadet Command. In 1993 the budget for EST was $3 million.

The results of Enhanced Skills Training have been remarkable. Arithmetic and algebra scores rose 17 percentile points, and reading scores by an astonishing 26 points. Of the students who completed the EST program, 99 percent passed the Officer Basic Course, the screening program that all new second lieutenants take after commissioning. Before EST, the success rate was about 80 percent. In other words, young black men who were identified as academically deficient were able, after remedial action, to perform at an extraordinarily high level.

The lesson of Enhanced Skills Training at HBCUs is twofold. First, a forthright acknowledgment of educational deficiencies must precede an effective program to bring individuals up to the required standards. Second, academic weaknesses revolve around basic subjects—reading, writing, and mathematics—where skills are needed not only for a military commission but also for any position of responsibility.

One other comment on HBCUs is in order. At a time when elite white schools are pursuing black entrants more than ever before, for many black students the role of the HBCU will be hard to replicate. Retired Brigadier General Clara L. Adams-Ender, a graduate of North Carolina A&T, relates:

> One thing a HBCU teaches you is how to be proud of your race and how your race can be proud of you. There is a close support system that is hard to come across at a white school. When I was taking my nurse's training at the University of Minnesota, there were fifty of us women there. Only one other besides myself was black. The nursing program was having a social event and she asked me if I was going to attend. I told her: "Woman, we have to go. Otherwise we'll be missed and everybody will think it's a racial statement!" Sometimes you want to be unnoticed and that is also what makes an HBCU attractive.

Raising High School Graduates to West Point Standards

The U.S. Military Academy at West Point remains the most prestigious source of commissions in the Army. About one

Army officer in five and three generals in ten are products of West Point. In 1993, 84 blacks were part of the incoming class of 1,212, 6.8 percent of the total. Forty percent of these were products of one of the most unusual secondary schools in America—the U.S. Military Academy Preparatory School (USMAPS). Without the "Prep School," as it is also known in Army circles, the number of black cadets would be perilously low.[6]

The Prep School was founded in 1916, when Congress authorized the Army to nominate enlisted men as cadets at West Point. Because many of these nominees did poorly on the service academy entrance examinations, slots at West Point reserved for enlisted men went unfilled. In response, the Army created preparatory schools on various posts to coach enlisted nominees for the entrance examinations. In 1946 the preparatory school program was established formally as a single independent military organization. Today, the U.S. Military Academy Preparatory School is located at Fort Monmouth, New Jersey. A colonel, usually a USMAPS alumnus, commands the school.

In 1994 the Prep School enrolled about 300 students. About half came from the junior enlisted ranks of the active Army. About a quarter were recent high school graduates who had applied to West Point, came close to meeting its standards, but who had not been accepted. Another quarter were recruited as athletes, identified by academy athletic departments. All cadet candidates must be no more than 21 years old when entering West Point. In recent years about 20 percent of the Prep School students have been black.

Of the 300 students admitted to the Prep School class of 1992–93, 200 completed the program, and 190 were recommended to West Point. (An attrition rate of about a third is normal.) The Military Academy accepted 176 of these nominees, who made up about a sixth of all West Point plebes (freshmen). Prep School graduates who are not admitted to

West Point are shifted informally to ROTC programs on university campuses, usually with four-year scholarships.

The Prep School does not charge for tuition, room, or board. Students who enter from enlisted duty are paid at the grade they earned before enrolling. Students who enter straight from high school are enlisted into the Army Reserve and receive the same monthly stipend as a West Point cadet—about $550 a month. Technically, such reservists incur a military obligation, but it is waived for dropouts from the Prep School. All students wear Army uniforms.

Results of the ten-month course of studies, essentially a fifth year of high school, are impressive, particularly for black students. Among black USMAPS alumni who entered West Point in 1991, 94 percent graduated with their class four years later. For comparison, 79 percent of the entire population of West Point matriculants graduated within four years in the class of 1995. Put another way, black USMAPS alumni admitted to West Point have a higher graduation rate than white "direct-admits" from civilian high schools without prior military service. Black West Point cadets who have not attended USMAPS, by contrast, normally lag behind their white peers. In the class of 1995, for example, only 77 percent of blacks admitted through normal procedures graduated.

The real success story of the Prep School is found among the prior enlisted soldiers. Nearly all had benefited from a kind of sponsored mobility—an officer or a first sergeant took interest in a young person with potential for leadership but weak academic credentials. The enlisted "prepsters," as they are known at West Point, earned higher grade-point averages than did the direct-admit applicants, even though they started out with lower Scholastic Aptitude Test (SAT) scores and high-school rankings. This pattern is most pronounced among black prepsters who had served a year or two of active military service.

One of the black students at the Prep School related his story:

> I never got into trouble, but I never really studied in high school either. If it wasn't for the Army I don't know where I'd be today. I was the company commander's driver and this gave us plenty of time to have long talks—about my plans, my future. He sent me to the education counselor and I took the written exam. One thing led to another, and here I am. It was tough at first, but now I know how to study. Math doesn't scare me anymore. I'm looking forward to being a company commander myself some day.

The success of the Military Academy Preparatory School seems to grow out of its intense concentration on basic skills and low ratio of staff to students. Another factor is its regimented atmosphere, including rigorous physical conditioning and orientation to military life, where Afro-Americans are very comfortable in the overall atmosphere of the Military Academy Preparatory School.

USMAPS is unapologetic about its narrow curriculum and its three-tier placement or tracking system, based on periodic diagnostic tests. Students are grouped at one of three levels: advanced, standard, or fundamentals. The advanced track is taught more calculus than the standard track. Students placed in fundamentals receive the same algebra and geometry coverage as those in the standard track but do not move on to matrices. Because USMAPS is so heavily academic in English and mathematics and does not offer the usual variety of courses, the Prep School is not accredited. As Colonel James Orahood, the USMAPS commander in 1994, put it: "Our curriculum is simple. We got English. We got math."

Prep School classes are small, an average of 15 students per teacher in a class. Schoolwide in 1994, a typical class of 300 students stood to benefit from the services of 63 staff members—20 officers, 23 enlisted soldiers (including 9 cooks), and 20 civilians. The teaching faculty is 16 strong— 5 military officers and 11 civilians.

USMAPS attempts to acclimate its students to military life in general but especially to life at the Military Academy. They memorize West Point calls and songs and learn the traditions of the academy. The biggest event of the year is the annual Army-Navy football game in Philadelphia, to which the whole school is bused.

As at West Point, students at the Prep School find themselves pressed for time and are under some pressure to partake, if not excel, in sports. Physical exertion and the time pressures serve to minimize invidious comparisons between students in fast and slow academic tracks. The school has an honor code, but, unlike West Point, it is administered by staff instead of fellow students. Also, again unlike West Point, there is no hazing.

A typical "cadet candidate" day begins with a wake-up call at 5:30 A.M. and ends with taps at 11:00 P.M.:

Time	Activity
05:30	First call
06:00–07:15	Breakfast
07:15	Second call
07:30–12:00	Academic classes
12:00–13:00	Lunch
13:00–15:30	Academic classes
15:30–17:30	Free time
17:30–19:00	Dinner
19:00–20:00	Personal prep time
20:00–23:00	Study in barracks
23:00	Taps

Because the military environment places people on a "more equal" footing and because black history and black culture are part of the larger ambiance of Army life, Afro-

Americans are comfortable at the Prep School. In the USMAPS office of one black "tactical officer"—a blend of adviser, role model, and disciplinary officer—a visitor sees on the wall pictures of General B. O. Davis, Jr.; of Henry Flipper, the first black graduate of West Point; and of the buffalo soldiers. At USMAPS black identity merges easily with Army identity.

One other feature of the Prep School also deserves mention: its effort to instill in its cadets an element of spirituality. In contrast to the West Point motto, "Duty, Honor, Country," the Prep School's motto is "Desire, Faith, Effort." The Heritage Room, where the history of the Prep School and its graduates is commemorated, was described to a visitor as a "somber place to make the student know that he is part of something bigger." The graduation talk is often given by the West Point chaplain.

Despite their successes in producing qualified entrants for West Point, the military preparatory schools have drawn criticism from outside agencies. These criticisms fall into three areas: the attrition rate is too high, too many athletes are recruited, and, most serious, the program is simply too expensive. Each of these points deserves comment.

As for attrition, the Prep School is in a double bind. It could reduce attrition easily, by not accepting the high-risk applicants. Colonel Orahood described the situation:

> We can always reduce attrition by simply making safe bets, but then we defeat the purpose of the school. We see ourselves as a school of opportunity for those who otherwise would not get in. But how do you explain this to the number crunchers?

The recruitment of athletes is also cause for concern. It is a source of justifiable pride that USMAPS graduates are more likely to matriculate at West Point than direct admits. This is not the case for Prep School athletes, however, who have a higher attrition rate from West Point than other cadet groups. Also, recruited athletes have a higher attrition rate at the Prep School itself. The recruitment of athletes is actually a function of the Military Academy, however, not the Prep School, and it is not an essential feature of USMAPS. As long as the service academies are expected to field stellar athletic teams, the preparatory schools will probably serve a feeder function. Instead of closing USMAPS because of athletic recruitment, it would be better to eliminate that part of its mandate.

Still, this issue must be placed in context. The proportion of USMAPS athlete graduates, 15 percent, is almost the same as the proportion of direct-admit athletes into West Point, and even direct-admit athletes have a higher attrition rate than nonathletes. Also important, and contrary to what one might think, Afro-Americans at the Prep School make up no greater proportion of the athletes than of the total student population.

The most common source of criticism of the Prep School is the cost: $40,000 to $60,000 per student per year, depending on who does the figuring.[7] As a benchmark, the average annual cost of a cadet at the Military Academy is $60,000. This figure is contrasted frequently with the cost of $25,000 or so to send a young person to a selective four-year college. Again, however, some context is needed. The tuition and fees charged by colleges come nowhere near meeting the true expenses; many of the costs are covered by endowment earnings and research grants from foundations or the government. Still, we must acknowledge that the military prep schools do not come cheap. We simply believe their accomplishments justify their expense.

The expenditures produce impressive results, especially for minority students. The average SAT score for a direct-admit West Point cadet is around 1250; to be considered seriously, an applicant should not score below the low 1100s.

The average white student entering the Prep School has an SAT score of 1030, blacks enter with an average of 970. By the end of the course of instruction, the average SAT score has risen 100 points for whites and 120 points for blacks.

Even so, pressures to replace USMAPS with contracts to civilian prep schools were growing. Surely, such private contracts would save money. Yet proposals to replace the Prep School with short courses in subjects where students need help miss the point. At the Prep School, basic mathematics and English skills are strengthened measurably, and the cadets learn effective study habits for the first time in their lives. A civilian contract program is not as likely as USMAPS to withstand pressures to cut attrition, which will inevitably lead to taking on only the safer cases. Also, and perhaps most fundamental, a civilian structure will be unable to replicate the comfortable racial atmosphere of the Prep School. Recall that 40 percent of incoming black students enter West Point by way of USMAPS. Without the Prep School the number of Afro-Americans at the Military Academy would be small indeed.

The costs are high because the Prep School is a total institution. The student is accountable in every way: personal, academic, athletic, and military. Also, the Prep School has that unquantifiable variable: the mystique of West Point. Many young people, who would not otherwise have a chance, are able to show their true merits. Many of them are destined to become senior officers in the Army. This is an American achievement story of no small import; one that ought not to be lost in abstract cost-benefit analyses.

Opportunity + Hard Work = Success

All these programs demonstrate impressively how blacks need only receive opportunities in order to achieve. The

Army does not consider a need for "diversity" as a goal, the usual justification for lowered standards. Such debates in civilian society inevitably stigmatize applicants by raising doubts about their true qualifications. More bluntly, they raise questions about whether blacks can make the grade.

Christopher Jencks, one of America's most sophisticated students of the "underclass," notes two paradoxes in American race and class relations. One is that while many whites will treat blacks as equal if they "act white," few are prepared to treats blacks as equals if they "act black." Jencks ruefully notes that he can "see no good way of resolving this kind of cultural conflict."[8] The other paradox is that if discrimination can spur its victims to greater effort, it may help them economically, but if discrimination convinces its victims that effort is never rewarded, it makes them unable to work at all within the system.

Perhaps the Army does point the way out of these dilemmas. On the cultural conflict issue, white soldiers "act black" and black soldiers "act white" to a degree rarely found in civilian society. On the effects of discrimination, even when blacks believe they have to be "twice as good" as whites—as many black soldiers do—the correlation between effort and reward is strong enough for people to choose to go the extra distance.

There are no easy ways to upgrade students with academic weaknesses, but the programs described here—some expensive, some less so—offer lessons. First, they all emphasize reading, writing, and mathematical skills. Although they include physical training and a military ethos, the "three Rs" remain paramount. In addition, completion of the program has a direct and clear payoff: entrance into the Army, promotion to NCO ranks, an officer's commission, admission to West Point. In the end, there are no real losers among those who stay the course.

6

Army Values and Black Achievement

The Turners of the Washington, D.C., area are probably America's No. 1 service academy family, for all four of the Turner siblings—Major Henry Turner, Jr., Lt. Ingrid Turner, and Captains Eric and Michael Turner—have graduated from either the U.S. Military Academy at West Point or the Naval Academy at Annapolis—a feat few families, whether Black or White, can match.

Ebony, May 1993, p. 7

Two features of Afro-American life too rarely receive notice. One is that blacks have a long tradition of achievement through higher education in the face of daunting racial discrimination—and often at tremendous personal sacrifice.

The other is that many black families have connections with military service spanning several generations. The black soldier today has become the primary pillar of black responsibility and attainment in both the Afro-American community and the larger society.

Let's look at the Kings and the Todds, two prominent black families whose histories and achievements are closely linked to the dual traditions of higher education and military service. Many other black families have similar histories.

Dr. John Q. Taylor King of Austin, Texas, is both the retired president of Huston-Tillotson, a historically black college, and a major general retired from the U.S. Army. By appointment of the governor, he is a lieutenant general in the Texas State Guard. Dr. King's father was an Army captain in World War I. His great-uncle served with the 10th Cavalry, one of the regiments of the famed buffalo soldiers in the nineteenth century. In 1866, Dr. King's paternal grandmother was in the first class that entered Fisk University, which became one of the most distinguished of the historically black colleges. When Dr. King himself graduated in 1937, he was the third generation of his family to have attended that college. All of his own children—physicians, professionals, and businesspeople—also went to Fisk University.

James H. Todd, Ph.D., is president of the Educational Resource Development Group in Oakland, California. Dr. Todd served in the Army for nine years, reaching the grade of sergeant first class before being disabled in Vietnam. He then embarked on a second career, spreading civilian and military education to inspire entrepreneurship among inner-city black youth. His father, Prentiss O. Todd, served as a technical sergeant in the Pacific theater in one of the few integrated units in World War II. Dr. Todd's wife, Gigi, retired as an Army sergeant major and shares her husband's calling. Their son, Mark, currently in the Army, also anticipates a military career. Dr. Todd, a strong advocate of bringing back

the draft, states: "Military service, next to religious traditions, is the strongest sustained tradition in African-American life."

Education and the Black Bourgeois Tradition

Long before the civil rights movement, long before affirmative action, there was a black middle class in America. Characterized by a stable family life, members of the old black
bourgeoisie typically earned their living through small enterprises, the professions, or the clergy—the only avenues open
to them that were likely to provide a modicum of financial
stability. In this segregated environment, academic excellence was not only encouraged but also expected by a black
middle class that set the standard for all blacks. Its emphasis
on education and family values was buttressed by black
institutions—the church, communal organizations, busi-
nesses, and the military.

From the contemporary debate over the state of the black
family, we would hardly realize that the black bourgeoisie
exhibited the traits sociologists now recognize as typical of
minority entrepreneurial classes: a commitment to family stability and a deep and unswerving emphasis on education for
their children. Academics have described some ethnic communities—Jews, Greeks, Armenians, Chinese, Koreans—as
being "middleman" groups because they occupy the middle of
the economic system in their roles as merchants and service
providers. To convey an important difference between black
entrepreneurs and the immigrant groups that came later, we
employ the term "truncated middleman."[1] Prevented by Jim
Crow and other manifestations of white racism from developing clienteles outside their community, black middlemen had
to rely on their own community for their livelihoods to a
much greater extent than immigrant merchant groups.

Like their immigrant counterparts, however, black middlemen attached great importance to family responsibility and education. Indeed, the black bourgeoisie, more than any other group of Americans, placed a pronounced emphasis on the education of their children. Charles Johnson, examining records in the early decades of this century, thus reported that "lowly families of the matriculants spent up to the limits of their earnings" to send their children to college.[2]

The Afro-American self-help tradition is different from that of immigrant groups not only because it confronted a level of de jure and de facto racism other groups did not encounter but also because it appeared earlier. Well before the Civil War, an abundance of middle-class merchants and professional blacks—and a handful of wealthy ones—could be found in Philadelphia, New York, Cincinnati, and even New Orleans and Baltimore, both located within slave states. The evidence suggests that the antebellum black business enterprises may have catered to a more racially diverse clientele than did post–Civil War entrepreneurs, who were restricted to black communities because of Jim Crow. In any event, by the end of the nineteenth century, a recognizable black bourgeoisie could be found in any American community with a sizable black population.

The historical record makes clear that the push for mass education in the South was due to the efforts of the black middle class, not whites. County records, even before the Civil War, reveal that free blacks in the South placed a greater value on education than whites.[3] In the Reconstruction era immediately after the war, as noted by W. E. B. Du Bois, "Public education for all at public expense was, in the South, a Negro idea."[4] The principle of universal education based on local taxation and state obligation was not accepted by whites until after Reconstruction, and then only grudgingly. Well after Reconstruction, many white Southerners viewed public education as a subversive extravagance inspired by carpetbaggers.[5]

Not surprisingly, once public education was established in the South, black schools received only about half as much funding per student as white schools. It has been overlooked, however, that the black middle class augmented public school budgets with its own private funds. Because of these donated sums, certain black school systems received almost the same funding per student as the white schools, which received few, if any, private donations from whites.

In the North, Afro-Americans also played an important, though again largely untold, role in educational expansion. Northern blacks were in the vanguard of private education for blacks to provide sanctuary against racial hostility. In 1856 the African Methodist Episcopal (AME) Church founded Wilberforce University in Ohio, the first college owned by black Americans. By 1907 the AME Church, at tremendous cost, supported 22 colleges and vocational training institutes. The most extensive self-initiated educational program for blacks was instituted by the Afro-American Baptist Church. By 1909 the black Baptists had established 102 schools, mainly boarding schools at secondary and college level in 21 states as well as 5 schools in Africa.[6] Today, the few remaining black boarding schools find themselves increasingly popular and oddly contemporary, offering learning, discipline, and the comfort of an all-black community.[7]

Forced to turn inward to their own community, this self-help group developed an absolute respect for black institutions, which, after all, their forebears had built and cherished. It would be foolish to suppose that all was kindness and light in the segregated world of the truncated black middlemen. They lived hard lives, made harder by Jim Crow. Still, the evidence shows that they did not consider their institutions inferior in any way. This phenomenon, mainly southern, explains why many offspring of the black self-help group still proudly attend historically black colleges and universities. Indeed, until the 1960s, the large majority of black professionals came from this self-help group of Afro-Americans via the historically black colleges and universities. We must resist any temptation to become nostalgic about the segregated era, but we should not forget that the self-help tradition of the black middle class and its institutions was a barrier against social disintegration within the Afro-American community.[8]

Education, Self-Help, and the Black Career Soldier

Today, the descendants of the old black bourgeoisie make up only a small part of the Afro-American middle class, and in their place black career soldiers, and particularly black NCOs, have become the primary transmitters of the self-help value structure. In this regard we follow the lead of Andrew Billingsley, who argues, in *Climbing Jacob's Ladder*, that today's black career soldier is the functional equivalent of the old black bourgeois and the current repository of the traditional black values.[9] This tradition praises the benefits of self-sacrifice, education for its children, and the advancement of the race. Black soldiers and NCOs have become role models for working-class and poor Afro-Americans.[10] It is no coincidence that black southerners are the most disproportionately overrepresented group of any population in the Army's career force, more so than blacks from outside the South or whites from any region.[11] Black NCOs, like members of the black bourgeoisie of yesteryear, are among the few people today who are likely to apply the expression "a disgrace to your race" to admonish wayward young people. Indeed, in the popular culture, the black drill sergeant has become a new stereotype—firm, perhaps a little rigid, but always with the best interests of his charges in mind. Lou Gossett, Jr., epitomized this role in the movie *An Officer and a Gentleman* (1982).

Based on anecdotal evidence, indirect data, and our own observations, service in the Army provides many of the same tangible moral and emotional benefits to individual black families, and blacks in general, as those once provided by the traditions and resources of the old black middle class. On the most basic level, the children of black military families are likely to receive most of the ingredients necessary for a successful start in life. They are surrounded by blacks who are successful in their careers, know how to function within large bureaucracies, make decisions, and manage others. And they enjoy access to a worldwide educational system of good quality. Perhaps most important, these children are immersed in a value system that stresses achievement through legitimate effort—and through which effort is visibly, tangibly rewarded. It is no wonder that Shirley Bender, head of admissions at the University of Texas, says she has seen "few problems at the university with the matriculation of children from military families, especially if they are black. They tend to come in, be well focused, and complete their studies."[12]

We also have some quantifiable evidence on the educational attainments of the children of the career military compared with civilians. The Department of Defense has two school systems set up for the children of service members. The larger system is the Department of Defense Dependents Schools (DoDDS) that operates schools for the children of military personnel who are stationed overseas. Although most children of military families in the United States attend civilian high schools, the Domestic Elementary and Secondary Schools (DESS) exists for service members in more isolated military installations.

In 1994, the average SAT score for white students among the general population of the United States was 940; for blacks it was 741, a gap of nearly 200 points. Within the DoDDS, whites scored 945 on the average, compared with

804 for blacks. That significant differences persist between blacks and whites within the military dependents' schools cannot and should not be overlooked. Nonetheless, the difference between the white and black students in the DoDDS system is markedly narrower than it is among the general student population. The SAT scores for the DESS are even more notable: blacks score 854 and whites 943. (The number of blacks taking the SAT in DESS is small, however: some 25 blacks and 90 whites per year, whereas the number in DoDDS is twenty times more.)

These comparative SAT scores lead to several conclusions. One is that white students perform about the same whether they are enrolled in civilian schools or Defense Department schools. Another is that black students who are enrolled in Defense Department schools perform much better than their civilian counterparts. In fact, the average score (804) attained by black students enrolled in DoDDS exceeds the score (786) of black students in civilian schools whose parents have bachelor's degrees. That the children of black sergeants generally outperform children from black civilian households higher up on the socioeconomic ladder is worthy of some note.

It is also revealing that the proportions of DoDDS high school seniors who plan to go directly to college are almost the same for the two races: 69 percent for whites and 64 percent for blacks. Outside the DoDDS, the percentage of black students who go to college is only slightly over half the rate of white students.

Taken together, the various indicators of higher academic achievement among black children from military families, compared with their civilian counterparts, support the proposition that military service bestows many of the same benefits that the old black middle class did in earlier times. In some ways, the benefits are purely practical. Children of military families are likely to have access to better schools than those available to the average black student in civilian life. At the same time, the adherence by career military soldiers to self-help values cannot help but be reflected in the performance of their children. Even children who attend the finest schools will not succeed unless their parents emphasize academic achievement.

Veterans

The direct and indirect benefits enjoyed by the families of Army personnel are not the only reasons military service is advantageous to blacks. The benefits gained by service members at the end of their enlistment are also important. The postservice attainments of Americans who have served in the military, compared with those who have not, are a matter of ongoing inquiry and debate. What may have been true in peacetime may not be true in war; what World War II veterans may have experienced may not apply to veterans of later wars; what may apply to conscripted forces may not apply in an all-volunteer era. Even so, just about all researchers agree that black veterans fare better than their nonveteran counterparts, all other things being equal.[13]

Across the board, World War II veterans did better than their nonveteran peers, as measured by subsequent education and earnings.[14] Individuals with the least education upon entering the service achieved the most benefits. Overall, military service had a positive impact amounting to an extra year of formal education for whites; for blacks, the equivalent effect was two or three additional years. Military service was most effective in raising the level of formal education desired after soldiers left the Army. This effect was strongest for southern blacks, followed by northern blacks, northern whites, and southern whites. In brief, military service during World War II not only raised aspirations but also—through the military experience itself, through the GI Bill, or through a combination of the two—helped to fulfill those aspirations.

Another revealing fact illustrates the special significance of military service among Afro-Americans. About half of all black men who were of age served in the military during World War II. An examination of this cohort in *Who's Who Among Black Americans* shows that 68 percent of the entrants had such military service. For civil rights activists, the proportion is 22 percent; for businessmen, 81 percent.[15] In other words, military service was a widespread experience among successful black businessmen, but relatively uncommon for civil rights activists. We are perplexed by this discrepancy, though it may be due to a disproportionate number of activists being clergymen, and hence exempted from military service.

The most carefully crafted research on the experiences of veterans who served in the 1960s and 1970s was conducted by Harley L. Browning, Sally C. Lopreato, and Dudley L. Poston, Jr., a team of sociologists at the University of Texas.[16] They found that white veterans with a high school education fared about the same in civilian life as their nonveteran counterparts, but that military service had a strong, positive effect on men who had not finished high school. They also found that blacks and Hispanics at all educational levels benefited most by veteran status. Blacks who returned to civilian life after being honorably discharged earned substantially more than blacks who had not served in the military.

This finding deserves comment because soldiers in general and black soldiers in particular do not usually leave the military with skills readily transferable to the civilian marketplace. Instead, as the authors of the Texas study say, the military functions as a "bridging environment" where the less educated and members of minorities acquire social skills and experiences that help to integrate them into the labor force. The military seems to teach deprived youths how to cooperate, how to accept authority, and how to cope with the bureaucratic complexity of large organizations. Further, military service may act as a screening device for prospective employers of minorities who assume that persons who have served successfully in the military can do so in civilian enterprise. Paul McClaine, a human resource manager for State Farm Insurance Companies, points out that "ex-military people bring to the job the experiences and stability of a past career."

We believe there is more to the story. The interracial leveling in military service gives black soldiers a perspective on society that is less easily acquired by black nonveterans. Simply to have completed a tour of duty means that a black soldier has competed, and competed successfully, with whites. The Army experience emphasizes the correlation between reward and effort (as opposed to reward and race). As a black sergeant stated: "The Army showed me that life can be hard no matter what your color. No race has it easy." That realization surely accounts for some of the intangible advantage that black veterans take away from military service.

Studies of veterans from the era of the all-volunteer force are consistent with earlier findings. The large majority of soldiers, both black (88 percent) and white (86 percent), view their military service in positive terms.[17] More Afro-American veterans, however, see themselves as having benefited from their Army service than do white veterans. Blacks are about half again more likely than whites to rate their military experience high on specific dimensions such as self-pride, self-discipline, ability to make friends, development of job skills, and ability to work with others.

Especially telling are the effects of military service on attitudes toward racial integration and separatism. An analysis of a national sample of black adult males shows that blacks with military backgrounds—particularly combat veterans—express much lower levels of separatist racial sentiments than do black nonveterans.[18] Because the veterans in the sample had served in the Vietnam era, they typically entered the military as draftees or as draft-motivated volunteers, which reduces the significance of self-selection factors as an explanation for this phenomenon. Our reading of the data suggests strongly that the military experience itself reduces the appeal of black nationalism in later life.

Significantly, the only study on the long-term effects of military service on white racism shows a different pattern. Racial attitudes of white veterans and nonveterans did not differ significantly, although veterans were more likely to have black friends than nonveterans.[19] The white veterans, nevertheless, were more likely to have black friends than the white nonveterans.

Attitudes of Blacks and Whites, Civilians and Soldiers

Blacks in the Army are more likely to hold conservative social values than either whites or blacks outside the military, though they are not as conservative as whites in the military. This results in part from the value structure of the Army, which emphasizes and rewards hard work and self-sufficiency and therefore reduces the likelihood that soldiers will subscribe to notions of victimization. This is yet another example of how blacks in the career military are similar to the old bourgeoisie, which almost instinctively sought to help itself when faced with adversity.

In earlier chapters we examined similarities and differences in attitudes among black and white soldiers. The overarching finding was that Afro-American soldiers were more likely than white soldiers to see racism in the military system, but they were also more likely to compare the military

TABLE 6.1

Work Satisfaction (Percentage Satisfied)

| | Civilians | | Soldiers | |
	Black	White	Black	White
Men	23	40	46	52
Women	25	41	47	46

Sources: Civilian data from *General Social Survey*, University of Chicago, National Opinion Research Center, 1991, ages 18 to 35: black N = 118, white N = 873. Army data from 1993 survey: black N = 1,282, white N = 1,824.

favorably with civilian life. Here we present attitudinal data of a different sort: a comparison of black and white soldiers with black and white civilians responding to the same questions employed in large-scale public opinion polls as well as surveys of university students.

As summarized in table 6.1, white soldiers are somewhat more likely than white civilians to be satisfied with their work. Black soldiers, however, are twice as likely as black civilians to be satisfied. Indeed, black soldiers are more satisfied with their jobs than white civilians. The patterns are about the same for men and for women of both races. We suspect that the comparatively greater job satisfaction reported by military blacks results from their conviction that their work will be rewarded, the reduced likelihood of their consignment to the least prestigious work (as occurs in civilian life), and the self-esteem imparted to soldiers for even the lowliest military tasks. Perhaps most striking here is the low level of job satisfaction among black civilians.

Table 6.2 reports attitudes dealing with family values. One item assessed attitudes on the statement: "Family life suffers when a woman has a full-time job." It may be no great surprise that soldiers of any race or sex are more likely than civilians to agree with this "traditional" assertion. Less expected, however, is the finding that black male soldiers are three times as likely as black civilian men to agree. Even

TABLE 6.2

Family Life (Percentage Agreeing)

	Civilians		Soldiers	
	Black	White	Black	White
Family life suffers when woman has full-time job:				
Men	10	31	29	40
Women	21	39	23	45
Divorce is too easy:				
Men	47	66	58	73
Women	44	59	61	72

Sources: Civilian data from *General Social Survey*, University of Chicago, National Opinion Research Center, 1991, ages 18 to 35: black N = 118, white N = 873. Army data from 1993 survey: black N = 1,282, white N = 1,824.

black female soldiers are about twice as likely as black civilian women to give the traditional response. Table 6.2 also reports survey data on another item tapping family values: "Divorce is too easy." The same pattern appears again. Soldiers, black and white, are more conservative than civilians on items that tap family values. The relevant point, however, is that the difference between soldiers and civilians is far greater for blacks than for whites.

Views on the causes of poverty are another indicator of basic social values. Table 6.3 displays comparisons of undergraduate students at Northwestern University with Army soldiers. These data are interesting because we are comparing two groups of similar age but of quite different social backgrounds: upper middle-class students and blue-collar soldiers.

As expected, students of both races, but especially blacks, are likely to give the more "liberal" response. That is, they view poor people as victims of unfair treatment and discrimination. Also not unexpectedly, white soldiers are the most likely to give the "conservative" response, agreeing that poor people "haven't really tried hard enough to improve."

TABLE 6.3

Poverty, Personal Responsibility, and Racial Harmony
(Percentage Agreeing)

	Students		Soldiers	
	Black	White	Black	White
1. *Most of the people who suffer from poverty:*				
❑ are victims of society's unfair treatment and discrimination	67	49	47	14
❑ haven't really tried hard enough to improve	10	28	37	61
❑ not sure	23	23	16	25
Total	100	100	100	100
2. *Since being (in the Army) (at this university), I get along with people of other races:*				
❑ better	9	18	25	38
❑ same as before	73	77	70	53
❑ worse	18	5	5	9
Total	100	100	100	100

Sources: 1993 Army survey: black N = 1,282, white N = 1,824. 1993 Northwestern survey by Laura L. Miller and Charles C. Moskos: black N = 89, white N = 542.

The salient finding here is that black soldiers occupy a middle position between the very liberal black undergraduates and the very conservative white soldiers. Indeed, the black soldiers are more likely than the white students to state that poor people have not really tried hard enough.

Yet despite the liberal values held by the Northwestern undergraduates, racial attitudes are much more favorable among the Army soldiers than they are among the supposedly more progressive students. Indeed, as also shown in Table 6.3, among the black students, twice as many reported that since arrival on campus they got along "worse" as got along "better" with people of other races. In contrast, black soldiers were five times more likely to say that their attitudes toward other races had become more positive than negative since they had entered the Army. Although differences between the white soldiers and the white students are less pronounced, the trend is the same: the races state they get along better in the Army than on the Northwestern campus. We have no reason to think these findings would be different at other universities. We trust that these data will convince readers that social conservatism is not inconsistent with improved race relations.

One other illustration of civilian-military contrasts in racial attitudes makes the point in a different way. The chasm between how blacks and whites see certain corners of American society shows up in the survey numbers on O. J. Simpson's guilt or innocence in the murder of his wife. A July 1994 Gallup Poll revealed strong differences between the races. Black Americans were four times as likely as whites to think Simpson was "definitely" or "probably" innocent. Indeed, these results became the subject of much editorial commentary when the Simpson trial became yet another one of those litmus-test issues that divide Americans by race.

We were able to include the identical Gallup Poll item the same month in a survey administered to American soldiers

TABLE 6.4

O. J. Simpson's Guilt or Innocence, July 1994 (Percentages)

	White		Black	
	National	Soldiers	National	Soldiers
Definitely or probably guilty	68	64	24	48
Not sure	17	19	16	23
Definitely or probably innocent	15	17	60	29
Total	100	100	100	100

Sources: National sample from Gallup Poll, July 1994; Army data from July 1994 survey by Laura L. Miller and Charles C. Moskos: black N = 56, white N = 142.

in Germany. As reported in table 6.4, no real differences appear between white soldiers and white civilians on the Simpson question. Although black soldiers were more likely than white soldiers to think Simpson innocent, the racial differences were much less marked in the military than in the national sample. Again, as in the question on poor people's efforts to improve themselves, black soldiers occupied a middle position between the whites' responses and those of black civilians.

The results of our impromptu survey on the guilt or innocence of O. J. Simpson are consistent with all the available data dealing with race: attitudinal differences between blacks and whites, though not absent by any means, are much less pronounced in the Army than in our nation at large.[20] It is too easy to say that blacks and whites see the American criminal justice system through a racial prism. It is better to ask under what conditions the worldviews of the races can come closer together. The Army shows that black and white social attitudes become much closer in settings with shared experiences and genuinely equal opportunity.

Afro-American Attitudes Toward Military Service

Afro-American attitudes toward the armed forces are extremely diverse and often contradictory. In overstated terms, the black general public tends to have favorable views of the military, while the black leadership and intelligentsia tend to be more critical.[21]

Let us look first at the positive side. The black public regards the military as a secure place of employment and an honorable career in its own right. Military training is seen as a mechanism to instill discipline and often as a way to straighten out unruly youths. GI Bill benefits received after service are viewed as an avenue of upward mobility. Perhaps most salient, however, the military, especially the Army, is regarded as an institution truly committed to equal opportunity, where soldiers of all races are treated fairly. According to national surveys, black Americans are four times as likely as whites to state that opportunities for advancement are greater in the armed forces than in civilian life.[22]

A negative view of military service is more typically articulated by black civil rights leaders and cultural figures. According to the predominant view in the civil rights establishment, defense spending takes federal funds away that might be spent on domestic social needs. Yet the antipathy to the armed forces runs deeper and arises from something more than competition for funding. *Boyz 'n the Hood* (1991), the acclaimed movie by black director John Singleton, is one example. The story is set in inner-city Los Angeles; the strong, favorably portrayed male lead character discourages a youth who wants to join the Army by saying, "A black man ain't got no place in the Army. A man can't be a man because you'll be doing the white man's dirty work."

The most commonly voiced complaint about black military service is that in the event of war Afro-Americans would suffer disproportionately. Although this belief, as shown earlier, is not borne out by the data, it continues to have widespread currency. Even if it were true, however, black leaders behave inconsistently, in the same breath voicing concern about the declining number of Afro-Americans serving in uniform in peacetime and worrying about high black casualties in wartime. This dilemma also appears in public opinion data: blacks are more likely than whites to say that there are both "too many" (21 percent versus 11 percent) blacks in the military and "too few" (32 percent versus 18 percent).[23]

We believe that the underlying opposition to military service among black civil rights leaders derives from another source. Much of this leadership was alienated from the long-term goals of American foreign policy during the Cold War, when resistance to Soviet expansion was central. Black civil rights leaders were not asked for their support; they did not seem to believe that Afro-Americans had a stake in broad defense issues. The same held true in the Gulf War. Not only did the civil rights leaders oppose sending troops to Saudi Arabia, but national surveys also showed that blacks were only half as likely as whites to say it was the right action to take.[24]

As the Cold War recedes, however, black attitudes on the use of American might abroad are changing. American blacks have become more supportive of overseas military intervention. The Congressional Black Caucus (CBC) applauded President George Bush's 1992 decision to send American troops into Somalia and even called on the United States to disarm the warlords. More notable was the strong CBC support for restoring Jean-Bertrand Aristide to the presidency of Haiti. Although the CBC ultimately was divided on the 1994 military intervention, it forced the Clinton administration to give the return of Aristide a high priority that otherwise would not have existed. Indeed, observers identify the hunger strike of Randall Robinson, head of TransAfrica, as one of the factors that motivated President Clinton to intervene in Haiti. Survey data also reflect a new state of affairs. Where whites overwhelmingly opposed an invasion of Haiti, a plurality of blacks supported it.[25] Indeed, we may be entering an era in which blacks will become increasingly influential in foreign policy, especially as it involves Africa and the Caribbean.

Still, the longstanding strain in relations between the American military and the black civilian leadership cannot be denied. Vernon E. Jordan, Jr., one of America's most prominent black leaders and a past president of the National Urban League, inexplicably omits the military in a 1995 listing of institutions where black leadership has been prominent.[26] While executive director of the NAACP, Benjamin

0

Chavis characterized the presence of Afro-Americans in the
military as due to "an involuntary draft . . . what makes the
draft involuntary are the conditions within our communities: rise in poverty, rise in unemployment, rise in health
care costs."[27] Likewise, Cornel West in *Race Matters* men-
tions the military only once, describing it as "often the only
option" for black youth.[28] The statements of Chavis and West
are disconcerting because of their assumption that sensible
blacks or blacks with choices should steer clear of the armed
forces. Such a mindset is unwilling to acknowledge that the
large number of Afro-Americans in the armed forces might
be due, at least in part, to patriotism, to an appreciation of
the military lifestyle, or to recognition of the pivotal role the
military has played in the growth of the black middle class.

Our conversations with senior black officers suggest that
the alienation is mutual. When the Congressional Black Caucus issued a formal condemnation of the U.S. invasion of
Grenada, the reaction of a senior black general was typical:
"Why can't they support us just this once?" During the Gulf
War, another black general explained, "I just tune out the so-
called black leadership when it comes to anything military."

Most senior black officers are unimpressed with the black
civilian establishment, which they believe seeks advancement for blacks through racial politics or through supplica-
tion to benevolent whites. These black officers derive manifest self-esteem from their own rise to positions of immense
authority—without any special treatment.

In addition, black military leaders, as a group, are unques-
tionably less socially liberal than black leaders outside the
armed forces. It is no coincidence that Colin L. Powell, as
chairman of the Joint Chiefs of Staff, and General Calvin
Waller, as deputy commander of Desert Storm, both took
public stands against lifting the ban on gays in the military.
In this sentiment, they were probably closer to the Afro-
American mainstream than the black civilian leaders.[29]

Despite this conservative tendency, our own informal poll suggested that black officers and NCOs are much more likely than their white peers to vote Democratic. The fact is that blacks in the military, unlike whites, cannot forget their color. One career sergeant told us, "My wife said I should vote Reagan because the man gave me a raise. But my father made me promise I would never vote for anyone who kept the black man down. I kept my promise to my father."

General Colin L. Powell: A New Vista

The elevation of Colin Luther Powell to the chairmanship of the Joint Chiefs of Staff in 1989 was an epic event in American race relations, whose significance has yet to be fully realized. Powell's experience embodies, in many ways, the relationship between the black middle class and success within the military as well as black America's diverse and inconsistent attitudes toward military service.

The son of Jamaican immigrants, Powell was born in Harlem in 1937 and raised in the South Bronx. His father, who was active in the Episcopal Church, was a foreman in a clothing factory who supplemented his earnings by selling ladies' suits out of his apartment. Like black middle-class families of earlier times, the Powell extended family displayed an extraordinary faith in the efficacy of education, and Colin Powell's generation rewarded their parents' efforts. Colin's only sibling, Marilyn, was an elementary school teacher in California until her retirement. A first cousin, J. Bruce Llewellyn, is one of America's wealthiest black businessmen and the founder of a major black charitable organization. Other cousins include the chief designer at Republic Aircraft, a Ph.D. in psychology, a biochemist, two judges, an ambassador, and Barbara Watson, the first woman to serve as assistant secretary of state.

The family of Powell's wife, Alma, exemplifies much of the old black middle-class tradition of commitment to higher education. Alma's father, Robert C. Johnson, received his baccalaureate from Talladega College and a master's degree from one of the most prestigious of the historically black colleges, Fisk University, also Mrs. Powell's alma mater. He ended his career in education as the principal of Parker High School, one of the two black high schools in Birmingham, Alabama. Alma's mother, Mildred Bell Johnson, a prominent figure in black Girl Scouting and the Congregational Church, graduated from Kentucky State Teachers College. Her parents were both graduates of Berea College in Kentucky. Mildred's brother, George Bell, was the principal of Birmingham's other black high school.

After high school, Colin Powell enrolled in Army ROTC at City College of New York, where he joined other black youths who were products of stable families. "They were not busted up like families are now," Powell has said. "Most everyone had a family. They may have been living in tenements, but they were families. Everyone of us was watched over by a set of parents, and almost everybody had a set of aunts and uncles hanging around who would also watch over us."[30]

Upon graduation from college in 1958, Powell was commissioned a second lieutenant. His extraordinary military career progressed from service as a junior officer in Vietnam, where he was wounded, through a series of command and staff jobs culminating in his appointment as chairman of the Joint Chiefs of Staff and his command of allied operations in the Gulf War. Indeed, Powell became the most highly esteemed military leader in the United States since World War II. Public opinion polls since the late 1980s have consistently reported him as among America's most admired persons. In the fall of 1995, a veritable "Powell-mania" accompanied his flirtation with running for president and the sales tour for his autobiography.[31] He is the first black

American who has a realistic chance of becoming president of the United States one day.

On the subject of the numbers of blacks in the military, Powell's remarks to the 1991 national NAACP convention are enlightening. "I never apologize to anybody when we're accused of the disproportionate number of minorities who seek military careers. I am proud that we offer those kinds of opportunities. And who we should be challenging are those who do not provide those opportunities. You don't like disproportionate numbers in the military, then go tell business, go tell unions, go tell those in corporate life to provide the kind of opportunity we provide in the armed services."[32] Indeed, Powell believes that the military can have a powerful effect on black youth.

He strongly favors introducing Junior Reserve Officers' Training Corps (JROTC) into the high school curriculum as a program to instill discipline and give a sense of hope and patriotism to young people in the inner cities.[33] In a Powell-initiated policy, Congress in 1992 voted to increase the number of JROTC units from 1,500 to 2,900 by the school year 1996–97. In 1995 some 200,000 students were enrolled in the Army JROTC, 75,000 of them black.[34] Why, Powell has wondered, do "liberal school administrators and teachers claim that we [are] trying to 'militarize' education"?[35]

On "back to Africa," Powell says:

I support following your route back as in discovering your family's journey to America. But to suggest that you go back to Africa and try to find there something that you can't find here—I think that is something of an illusion. We have to live here and make our bed and our life here. If "here" is not good enough, then we've got to improve it.[36]

In a 1992 commencement address at Fisk University, Powell stated:

I want you to believe in America with all your heart, with all your mind, with all your soul, and with all your body. I've traveled around this world and I've seen a hundred countries, and I've got to tell you there is no better place or system on earth than that which we enjoy here in America.[37]

Precisely because of his prominence, Powell could also serve as an illustration of the contradictory images of the armed forces. The left-liberal political establishment regards Powell as a man who has distanced himself from the struggle of Afro-Americans. Film director Spike Lee dismisses Powell as an "Uncle Tom."[38] Jesse Jackson states that "very right-wing white people can trust him."[39] Andrew Hacker, a leading authority on American race relations who is white, criticizes Powell for not being black enough. Hacker asserts that Powell "put 99 percent of himself, of his black self, on hold, in the back because he was ambitious, wanted to get ahead and did."[40]

Hacker seems unaware that Powell has never shied away from his black identity. His office during his tenure as chairman of the Joint Chiefs prominently featured paintings of black regiments from the Civil War to World War II. Powell has long been a featured speaker on the black lecture circuit, especially at black colleges, and has been interviewed numerous times on issues of color. One of his frequent themes is to stress the black military heritage of America. Typical are Powell's remarks in his May 1993 commencement address at Howard University (where he became a member of the Board of Trustees in January 1996):

I stand here today as a direct descendant of those buffalo soldiers and of the Tuskegee Airmen and all the black men and women who have served the nation in uniform. I will never forget my debt to them. I didn't just show up. I climbed on the backs of those who never had the kind of opportunity that I had. I will never forget. You must never forget.[41]

Still, Hacker and other critics implicitly raise an important point: Is there a contradiction between having a "black identity" and being an American soldier—or, even more broadly, an American? In the Army, because there are so many black NCOs, Afro-American sergeants can be more culturally black than a black officer can be. A white faculty member at West Point states it this way: "Some black cadets want to maintain a distinctive identity through speech, gestures, and body language, and still be part of the officer corps. Actually, this is more difficult for officers than for the enlisted ranks. Black NCOs are strong role models and that makes it easier for an enlisted man to be black and a successful sergeant at the same time. A cadet who is too black is not going to hack it."[42]

Colin Powell points the way out of this dilemma. In a 1993 convocation speech at a predominantly black college in Birmingham, Alabama, Powell spoke of the "second civil war fought in the Sixties" to free Americans of racism. "You know the leaders of that second civil war—Martin, Thurgood, Jesse, Rosa, Andrew, and Cora, and hundreds of others who pledged their lives, their fortunes, and their sacred honor to achieve victory in that war."[43] This is black identity without the threat—no rage at whites, no talk about compensation for past injustices, no aching sense of victimization.

By fusing the imagery of the Declaration of Independence with the personages of the civil rights movement, by blending the black struggle with the identity of all Americans, Powell opens up a new vista where our country's Afro-American heritage and the totality of American history merge. This is one of the race lessons of the Army.

7

Army Lessons for American Society

We now turn our attention to whether the military's impressive experience in race relations might be extended to the rest of America. Those who wish to translate the military's racial successes into a nonmilitary setting run into a paradox. The purpose of the military, after all, is to defend the United States and its national interests—not to improve race relations. The Army succeeds as a remedial organization for many youths with otherwise dead-end prospects precisely because it does not define itself as a remedial organization. Any program established solely to better the lot of poor blacks (or poor whites), or to encourage salutary interaction between blacks and whites, would lack broad legitimacy and inevitably be marginalized. To be successful, a program must achieve its racial benefits as a by-product of some other purpose, and not as its manifest goal.

Analogies between military and civilian organizations naturally have limitations, especially in matters of race. After all, the armed forces are highly structured, and insights gained from their experience would seem to apply mainly to other large bureaucracies such as major corporations, the civil service, and educational institutions. Changes afoot in American society, however, seem to augur a decline in large bureaucratic structures. Big business may be giving way to small business, big labor unions are shrinking, and even big government has come under unprecedented attack. Perhaps the erosion of large bureaucratic structures signals the rise of a postindustrial middle class that more closely resembles the old middle class of self-employed and small employers.[1] In any event, structural changes in these directions further attenuate civilian analogies with race relations in the military.

Accurate comparisons between the military and civilian bureaucracies would be no small accomplishment. Yet despite the voluminous literature on race relations, little research has been done into the way racial opportunities work in large civilian organizations. One study of the corporate world and several on secondary schools do, however, permit some comparative analysis of black achievement. We can thus develop some analytical understanding of the way certain features of the military may well apply to the larger society.

From what we know, the race picture in large corporations is dismal. A comprehensive 1995 survey of senior executives in the highest corporate ranks revealed only six minorities out of every thousand.[2] Lawrence Otis Graham, in one of the best-conceived studies on corporations, dealt with firms with large minority representation at managerial levels. He defined "large" as at least 10 percent minorities—and this figure included all racial minorities, not just blacks.[3]

Graham's findings, though not specific to the military experience, reveal some interesting similarities between the corporate world and the armed forces. Corporations with large numbers of minority managers are most likely to offer in-house training programs for future advancement; such programs, though not targeted to minorities, are attended disproportionately by minority members. As in the Army's commissioning programs, corporate recruiting for management positions relies heavily on historically black colleges and universities. Like his counterparts in the Army, Graham believes that bringing blacks into the system is the first priority. Most important, Graham stresses that the rationale for hiring and promoting minorities in corporations is to achieve the organization's goals—increased profits—not as an end in itself. Graham also holds, significantly, that "diversity training" has little use in organizations that do not already have a respectable number of minority members.

We are extremely skeptical about "multicultural" education in settings with few or no blacks. Indeed, without a substantial black presence, such education can detract from blacks' opportunity by becoming a vehicle for other "oppressed" groups—women, Hispanics, Asian Americans, gays and lesbians, and so on. Because of the unique conditions of Afro-American life and history, the emphasis must remain on recruiting blacks and expanding their opportunities.

The unintended consequences of multiculturalism were revealed in an event at the University of Texas at Austin, where John Butler is on the faculty. After a racial incident on the campus, black students conducted a protest march. The administration responded with classes in diversity and sensitivity for faculty and students. The initial racial incident was pushed into the background as concern shifted from the problems confronted by blacks to those of white women, white gays and lesbians, and the handicapped. Butler, in exasperation and perhaps with some exaggeration, finally declared that he would prefer 10,000 black students on campus with 38,000 white racists to the status quo of 1,000 black students with 47,000 white students taking politically correct courses.

A successful venture to recruit poor blacks into previously almost all-white elite prep schools also suggests some analogies with the Army's success in raising black achievement. The ABC ("A Better Chance") program was founded in 1963 to increase the number of low-income minority students in independent preparatory schools. More than two-thirds of the enrollees were black; the remainder were Hispanics, Asians, and other people of color. Sixteen elite prep schools took part in the program. The major support came from the Office of Economic Opportunity (OEO), with supplementary funds from Dartmouth College, the Merrill Foundation, and the Rockefeller Foundation.

An excellent account of the process that allowed minority youths from deprived backgrounds to attend the finest secondary schools in the country has been given by Richard L. Zweigenhaft and G. William Domhoff.[4] It began with identification of students who had the potential for serious learning. Before departing for prep school, these students attended an eight-week summer orientation in a residential setting away from their home areas. On the assumption that academic excellence depends mainly on verbal and mathematical skills, the focus was on intensive English and mathematics. The academic work was supplemented by cultural activities and athletics as well as instruction in some of the "social graces."

Observers of black high school performance have noted what has been called an "oppositional identity." Many black students fight back against degrading racism and poverty by developing a cultural identity in which success in school is defined as "acting white," abandoning black social identity. In the ABC program such a self-defeating identity did not develop, partly because the students were moved out of their homes and neighborhoods. The authors' findings show some striking parallels with the social psychology of Army basic training:

> What the ABC program did very simply, was to negate the usual social-psychological dialectic between the powerful and the powerless by initiating its black students into a new social and psychological identity that overcame the effects of stigmatization and any inclinations toward an oppositional identity.[5]

More than four-fifths of the ABC students graduated from their prep schools. Virtually every one of them attended college, often the most selective in the country. ABC was an unusual success story—but for only four years. When the OEO funding ended in 1967, ABC underwent a fundamental shift, changing from a program designed to identify poor blacks who could be "prepped" for prep school to a program to help black middle-class parents enroll their children in private schools.

Another civilian educational parallel with Army values can be drawn from the experience of parochial religious schools. A careful study of Catholic high schools, for example, found that they are more racially diverse than public schools and produce better results for all students.[6] While acknowledging the differences in student selection between public and parochial schools, the study attributed successful education at the Catholic schools largely to an emphasis on communal organization over individual development and self-choice. In addition, faculty and students of parochial schools share a broad set of beliefs on how to conduct themselves and what kind of people they should become. The faculty regarded themselves not as specialists in academic subjects but as mentors and role models, and presented Jesus' preaching of God's kingdom and his death and resurrection as images to encourage struggles against poverty and injustice.

Although secular organizations cannot employ the imagery of religions, they can promote common values that emphasize communal responsibilities and deemphasize individual rights, as is done in the military. As James Fallows notes:

> Most agencies of the government have no special standing to speak about the general national welfare. Each represents a certain constituency; the interest groups fight it out. The military, strangely, is the one government institution that has been assigned legitimacy to act on its notion of the collective good.[7]

Again, we stress our belief that the most effective way to improve race relations in this country is to increase the number of blacks who have access to the tools necessary to compete on a level playing field and to bring whites and blacks together in a common cause.

The likelihood of a return to conscription appears to be virtually nil at this time, but we would still welcome a national debate about who serves when not all serve. Our concern here, however, is more sharply focused: How do we, without conscription, obtain some of the democratizing advantages of the draft? The equalizing effect prevalent in the American military organization can be replicated on a large scale only in national service, where intense cooperation is also required.

National service involves young people in performing duties that instill a sense of participation in public life by providing services recognized by the citizenry at large as needed. National service is not a jobs program; it is not an excuse for putting underprivileged or unemployed young people on the public payroll. Indeed, an essential feature of national service, as we see it, is that participants are paid a subsistence wage, in order to leave no question—in their own minds or in the minds of the public—that they are serving the country, and not profiting from a government job. To that end, the work performed by civilian servers should be of undeniable value to society—providing services that cannot be effectively delivered by market forces and that are too costly for the government to undertake otherwise. Valuable national service could be done in a variety of ways: working in conservation programs, staffing agencies to help old people to live on their own, bringing on new hands to help the institutionalized, and teaching English as a second language to immigrants, to name but a few.

These activities alone would be sufficient justification for a national service program. They are the main benefits the general citizenry would recognize and grow to value. A properly conceived national service plan would also replicate the benefits in race relations that are now limited basically to the military. Like the Army, a national service program could serve as a "bridging environment" for disadvantaged youth, teaching them how to take on responsibility, acquire productive habits, and perform needed work in a public organization.[8] Like the Army in modern times, national service would bring together, in a common cause, persons of diverse background and different races.

The military analogy has another lesson. In much the same way as the GI Bill has offered the promise of upward mobility for military veterans, postservice educational benefits for civilian servers would do the same. Our linchpin proposal is to extend to civilian service the educational and job training benefits principle of the GI Bill. This arrangement would move the nation away from the increasing reliance on student loans to cover the costs of higher education. By replacing student loan programs with GI Bill–type grants, the government would greatly increase young people's access to higher education through service. Linking national service to student aid would strengthen the constituency for student aid across all sectors of society.[9] Remember that in 1949 our country gladly spent 1 percent of the gross national product on the GI Bill for military veterans—$65 billion in today's dollars!

National service would open avenues as never before to deprived young people (local and state youth corps already show overwhelming enrollment by poor and minority youths). A national youth service corps, the functional equivalent of the draft Army, would offer an opportunity for college or vocational training to many young men and women who would otherwise be trapped in a dead-end existence. The original GI Bill offered many veterans a leg up; a civilian youth corps would do the same for the young today. In 1995, the first year of operation of President Clinton's AmeriCorps program, Afro-Americans constituted 31 percent of the membership: a figure almost identical with the proportion of blacks in the Army's enlisted ranks.

Our proposal would have another important advantage. By providing enticements likely to attract a large number of middle-class, college-bound youth, national service would preclude the debilitating, self-reinforcing stigma of programs targeted only toward poor youths. A comprehensive program of national service would call upon all of our country's races and classes to join in a common civic enterprise. If this possibility is ignored and if time is allowed to pass, the richest country in the world will enter the twenty-first century crippled by an unemployed and embittered underclass. The actual numbers make the point. During the peacetime draft years (1953–65) an average of 170,000 black men turned eighteen every year. About 65,000 of them entered the military annually. In 1995, about 265,000 black males turned eighteen, and 22,000 of them joined the armed services. If the same percentage of black men had entered the military in 1995 as during the peacetime draft, the figure would be around 100,000: well over four times the actual number. Put another way, if the draft that operated in the Cold War were still in effect, some 75,000 more black men would enter the military each year.

These are sobering statistics, given the historical importance of military service for creation of opportunities for black achievement: living a disciplined life, skill training for many, and postservice educational benefits. To our knowledge, the possibility that the growth of a black underclass might be connected in some way to the end of conscription has never been seriously proposed, much less examined. But this line of argument ought not be dismissed lightly. The only institution with any potential for taking up the slack created by the military drawdown is some form of civilian national service for young people.

The most extravagant expectations for national service will, of course, never be fulfilled. National service is not a panacea for all of society's problems, not even those directly associated with young people. The tangle of macroeconomic change, social pathologies, and racial marginalization that has produced an underclass youth will not unsnarl magically with the introduction of national service. Nonetheless, the service concept is the most promising of many proposals, and the one that comes closest to the military analogy. Although we must be careful not to succumb to the seduction of national service as a cure-all for America's social ills, we should accept and harness the transformational power that concentrated performance of civic duty can generate among the youths involved.

Afro-Anglo Culture as Core American Culture

The Army's multiracial uniculture—and the fact that this uniculture is Afro-Anglo—has been an unquantifiable contributor to its success in race relations. American society sorely needs some similar amalgamation of the two dominant cultures.

We use the term "Afro-Anglo" in a special sense. The "Anglo" refers to the British heritage that Americans, whatever their own ethnicity, recognize as the core of our country's culture: our language, our social customs, and especially our legal and political traditions. We must also recognize our culture's core "Afro" element: moral vision, rhetoric, literature, music, and a distinctive Protestant Christianity. Immigrants have also shaped our national identity, but the bedrock culture remains Afro-Anglo. Leaving aside black majority countries, few countries (Brazil? Cuba?) have been influenced as strongly by African culture as our own. To take an obvious example, black music—spirituals, gospel, blues, jazz, tap, ragtime, boogie-woogie, bebop, rap—has attracted appreciative audiences not only in the United States but throughout much of the world. It would be hard to overstate how strongly a numerically small racial minority has influenced a dominant racial majority, indeed the culture of the dominant nation on the world scene.

But the "Afro" component in our national culture is more profound than that recognized beyond our borders. Peter Kolchin and others have argued that slavery was the defining American institution, one that distinguished the English colonies from England.[10] Slave narratives were recognized as the first original genre of American literature, even before the Civil War.[11] In the nineteenth century, the genius of Herman Melville and Mark Twain was to grapple—either directly or through metaphor—with the moral problem posed by racial slavery in the heart of American democracy.

More to the point, many of what are considered the distinctive features of southern speech, originating in the era of slavery, are now seen to run from black to white, rather than the other way around.[12]

Important as slavery was, it is not the whole story of Afro-Americans. Afro-American religion has been termed the paradigm of American religion.[13] Blacks ennobled America with the promise of biblical salvation through racial comity. The syncretism of American black churches in Protestant America—based on Bible-centered preaching and on testimony—differs from the religious forms of the African diaspora in Catholic-dominated countries, such as voodoo, obeah, and Santeria.[14] Modern Pentecostalism, racially integrated but predominantly white, is today one of the fastest growing religious movements, both in the United States and abroad. Few people realize that Pentecostalism began in a Los Angeles black mission church in 1906.[15] In contrast to the secular side of American culture, black spirituality brings religious values and vocabulary into the public square.[16]

The very rhetoric of the American creed has been singularly shaped by Afro-American formulations of equality.[17] George Schuyler, one of this century's most penetrating black essayists, believed that we should not consider "Aframerican" art separate or distinct from American art. To do so would play into the hands of the white power structure, thereby limiting black writing to the margins of American society.[18] Our country's debt to Carter G. Woodson (1875–1950), the "father of Negro history," is enormous; his introduction of black history into American history has had great scholarly resonance. It has been argued plausibly that black culture gave Americans their own national form of humor.[19]

Some selective quotes illustrate this point of the centrality of Afro-American culture to the mainstream of America. Ralph Ellison wrote that blacks are at the center of America's complex hybrid culture rather than candidates to be included

within it: "Whatever else the true American is, he is also
somehow black."[20] Cornel West criticizes both liberals and
conservatives for failing to see that black people are "neither
additions nor defections in American life, but rather consti-
tutive elements of that life."[21] Nathan Huggins states: "Afro-
American history and American history are not only essential to one another. They share a common historical fate."[22]
In the words of Ishmael Reed, "There's no such thing as
Black America or White America, two nations, two separate
bloodlines. America is a land of distant cousins."[23] Lerone
Bennett, Jr., captures the core quality of black centrality in
America in the title of his magisterial history of black Amer-
ica, *Before the Mayflower*.[24]

The Army offers an important model for how we ought to
consider the Afro-American component in our culture. Black
history, instead of being held apart (as the multicultural
establishment seems to prefer), should be seen as an original
and shaping part of core American culture. Instead of a
multicultural view of America, we need a unified American
national identity whose core is recognized as Afro-Anglo.[25] A
group that for too long has felt alienated from what it imag-
ined to be the mainstream of American culture must now
realize that it has long been part of that mainstream.

In early 1995, feature stories for the *New Yorker* and the
Atlantic Monthly separately made the same point: America's
current public intellectuals are disproportionately black (as
they were disproportionately Jewish in the decades following World War II).[26] Black intellectuals and writers have been
active since the inception of the Republic—think of Frederick Douglass, Ida B. Wells, W. E. B. Du Bois, James Baldwin,
Gwendolyn Brooks, Ralph Ellison, Langston Hughes, Alice
Walker, and Toni Morrison, to name but a few of the best
known. Their works have, or should have, entered the
national canon. Even so, nothing before in our history has
approached the contemporary number of black writers, film

directors, commentators, and intellectuals who are at the center of debate on what American culture is all about.[27]

If America is to be truly a world leader, its message must not be empty of moral content. An invocation of our black heritage, which has deepened and enhanced the American dream, is as important as our economic and military might. Our own civil rights struggle has become part of the world movement toward freedom. John Hope Franklin, the dean of black historians, puts it succinctly: "The role of the Negro in America is not only significant in itself but central in the task of fulfilling the nation's true destiny."[28] The crux of American exceptionalism may well be the influence of black Americans on the total culture.

We do not know how to cause Americans to conceive of themselves as belonging to a single, Afro-Anglo culture, but emphasizing our differences and treating our ethnic groups as separate and distinct will not do it. Resolving this dilemma may disclose answers to far more of our racial problems than we can imagine.

★★

Overcoming Race: A Primer

How, then, do we transfer the Army's successes to nonmilitary settings? Differences between military and civilian settings preclude exact analogies, but we can articulate the key principles of the Army experience. In all of the lessons we shall list, social research can be invaluable. This has been demonstrated by the Army's long reliance on social scientists to ascertain attitudes on racial matters, steps to improve equal opportunity, and how such factors affect organizational performance.

★★ *Lesson One:* **Blacks and Whites Will Not View Opportunities and Race Relations the Same Way.**

Even in the Army, the most successfully racially integrated institution in American society, blacks and whites still have disparate views of equal opportunity. Blacks consistently take a dimmer view of racial matters than whites. This cuts across gender and rank. In no foreseeable situation in any American institution, much less in society as a whole, is this likely to change soon. Nevertheless, the Army shows that black and white social attitudes can become significantly closer in egalitarian settings with shared experiences. It also shows that blacks and whites do not have to hold identical views of the racial situation in order to succeed together.

★★ *Lesson Two:* **Focus on Black Opportunity, Not on Prohibiting Racist Expression.**

Civilian organizations, especially universities, try to improve the racial climate by eradicating racist statements and symbols. Such efforts are meaningful only when accompanied by concrete steps to expand the pool of qualified black students and faculty. Likewise, in governmental and corporate structures, the emphasis must continually be on opening avenues of opportunity for black participation and movement into leadership roles. Lamentable as the presence of white racists may be, it is not the core issue. Indeed, Afro-American history testifies eloquently that black accomplishment can occur despite pervasive white racism. It would be foolhardy to consider the absence of white racists as a precondition for black achievement. This is one of the most significant morals of the Army experience.

★★ *Lesson Three:* **Be Ruthless Against Discrimination.**

Formal efforts to prohibit racist expressions can be a way of avoiding a genuine opening up of channels for black advancement, but this realization does not imply that any retreat from antidiscrimination should be made. Racist behavior cannot be tolerated within the leadership of an organization. Individuals who display racist tendencies must not be promoted to positions of responsibility. In the Army, racist behavior ends a person's career. That racial remarks are rarely heard among Army NCOs and officers, even in all-white groups, reflects how strictly this norm is adhered to. Whether formal or informal, promotion criteria must include sensitivity on racial matters. Shelby Steele's proposal to criminalize racial discrimination (though not his proposal to do away with affirmative action) has, in a manner of speaking, been accomplished de facto in the military.[29]

★★ *Lesson Four:* **Create Conditions so That White and Black Youth Can Serve on an Equal Basis to Improve Their Social and Civic Opportunities.**

The intense cooperation required to meet military goals has a democratizing effect in the Army. Gordon W. Allport's long-standing and hard-wearing "equal contact" statement four decades ago remains a classic:

Prejudice ... may be reduced by equal status contact between majority and minority groups in the pursuit of common goals. The effect is greatly enhanced if this contact is sanctioned by institutional supports ... and provided it is of the sort that leads to the perception of common interests and common humanity between members of the two groups.[30]

Some form of civilian national service is the only likely means of restoring the opportunities for young people that were reduced by the end of conscription and further limited by the military drawdown. The connection between the demise of the draft and the growth of an underclass is a plausible hypothesis and deserves examination. The critical point is that sharing the obligations of citizenship will act as a solvent for many of the differences among national servers. That all participants will live at not much more than subsistence levels and that all will be equally eligible for post-service educational benefits underscore the egalitarianism of the national service proposal. We encourage a public debate about the merits of youth service in either civilian or military capacities, whether compulsory, voluntary, or benefit-contingent.

The GI Bill following World War II was a remarkable success, a social experiment that led to a broad, lasting, and most positive impact in America. National service linked to a GI Bill principle—benefits premised on service, not need—would result in much the same democratizing effect that has traditionally occurred among military members. Precisely because many young people from across the social spectrum would participate—if not shoulder to shoulder, then at least under one large umbrella—invidious stereotyping would be kept to a minimum. As in the military, the emphasis must be on the service performed and not on the server. The GI Bill continues to serve as the best model to engender true equality of opportunity. A comprehensive sociological study completed in 1996 shows that an "away from home" experience, as traditionally accompanies military service, coupled with generous GI Bill benefits, dramatically improves the life chances of the youths who were most disadvantaged prior to entering the armed forces.[31]

★ ★ Lesson Five: Install Qualified Black Leaders as Soon as Possible.

The quickest way to dispel stereotypes of black incapacity is to bring white people into contact with highly qualified Afro-American leaders. In the Army, this contact is likely to occur on the first day and to continue throughout the term of service. Again, we stress that only in the Army are whites routinely bossed by blacks.

Historically black colleges and universities (HBCUs) play a large but underappreciated role in forming Afro-American leaders in a variety of fields. These institutions of higher education produce close to half of all black officers in the U.S. Army. In a sociological context, HBCUs show how two seemingly opposing goals—racial integration and strengthening black institutions—reflect the same movement toward an inclusive, shared American national identity.

Without a critical mass of blacks, as exists in the Army, the beneficial effects of equal opportunity for leadership roles are difficult to realize. Although the number that constitutes a critical mass cannot be specified with exactitude, the lower range probably approximates the number of blacks in the American population—around one in nine. It may be time to rethink the advisability of historically white and elite colleges' competing against each other for qualified black students and faculty.[32] Better, perhaps, would be policies for such blacks to accumulate in greater numbers in fewer selected institutions, thus building the critical mass that has allowed historically black schools to produce a disproportionate share of high achievers. We view affirmative action in college admissions as one of society's mechanisms to equalize opportunity, not as part of the reward system for achievement.

✪★ *Lesson Six:* **Affirmative Action Must Be Linked to Standards and Pools of Qualified Candidates.**

The Army eschews promotion quotas, but it does set goals. These goals are based on the racial composition of the relevant pool of qualified candidates, not on the proportion of blacks in the entire organization, much less on general population figures. Failure to meet goals must be explained, but "timetables" do not exist. This "soft" affirmative action contrasts with the quota-driven programs that have characterized federal agencies.[33] Indeed, the earlier noted promotion lag of blacks compared to whites at certain levels, especially from captain to major, indicates that Army promotions are not bound to goals.

Maintenance of common standards for promotion may cause short-term turmoil, as it did in the Army of the 1970s, but it also means that individuals who attain senior positions are fully qualified. Any set of standards must also take into account, as does the Army, such "whole-person" qualities as initiative, perseverance, leadership, and commitment to organizational goals. That the Army contained few putative liberals willing to rationalize an initial drop in standards allowed blacks who were promoted in the early days to become the strongest defenders of standards for their own black subordinates. An organization that promotes the less qualified to buy temporary peace only invites long-term disaffection.

★ ★ *Lesson Seven:* **Affirmative Action Must Follow a "Supply-side" Model, Not a "Demand-side" Model.**

In practical terms, the Army has developed an affirmative action program based on "supply." This contrasts with the typical "demand" version of affirmative action, where goals and quotas are set before attempting to enlarge the pool of qualified people.

The Army shows that youths with deficient backgrounds can meet demanding academic as well as physical standards. The Army's internal programs bring young people up to enlistment standards, enlisted soldiers to noncommissioned officer standards, undergraduates to officer-commissioning standards, and high school graduates to West Point–admission standards. These programs are not targeted exclusively to minority soldiers, but the participants are disproportionately Afro-American.

Here we interject an object lesson on an affirmative action program—one based on the demand-side model—that seems destined not to work. In 1995, the Navy announced a "12/12/5" goal for the year 2000. By that date, the Navy wants to attain an officer accession that is at least 12 percent black, 12 percent Hispanic, and 5 percent Asian or Pacific Islander.[34] (In time, that figure is supposed to become the standard for the total officer composition.) Reaching that goal means the percentage of officer accessions in the designated racial categories would have to triple within five years. Asked about the origin of the "12/12/5" figure, a very senior Navy official told us it was the projected racial composition of the United States and the "Navy should look like America." Toward this goal, the Navy has introduced initiatives that allow recruiters some leeway in offering Navy ROTC scholarships to minority applicants.[35] Yet the Navy goals are untenable unless accompanied by new programs to expand the pool of minorities who could be raised to meet commissioning standards. Unlike the Army, for example, the Navy has a small presence in the ROTC programs in historically black colleges.[36] In the light of the Navy's insistence that standards "will not be dropped," the Navy's "12/12/5" goals appear unrealistic.

The lesson here is simple: diversity in and of itself is not a rationale for affirmative action. Indeed, under the 1995 Supreme Court ruling in *Adarand Construction v. Peña*, affirmative action for the purpose of reflecting racial and ethnic diversity for its own sake is unconstitutional. It is much better to build up avenues of equal opportunity than to concoct numbers to correspond with notions of diversity based on gross population numbers.

★★ *Lesson Eight:* **A Level Playing Field Is Not Always Enough.**

The evaluation of programs to boost academic skills and test scores is fraught with difficulty. But "intelligence"—as measured by achievement tests—can be raised impressively through programs that are well staffed, have motivated participants, and use a military regimen. Residential programs away from the participants' home area seem to be the most effective way to resocialize young people toward productive goals. As in the Army, skill-boosting programs should emphasize mathematics, reading, and writing. These programs cost money and require a big commitment of resources; they also visibly pay off for those who complete them.

Good affirmative action acknowledges that members of disadvantaged groups may need compensatory action to meet the standards of competition. Bad affirmative action suspends those standards. Always, the objective should be to prepare members of a historically disadvantaged population to compete on an equal footing with the more privileged. Sometimes, as in the Army's remedial programs, "throwing money" at a social problem does solve it.

★ ★ *Lesson Nine:* **Affirmative Action Should Be Focused on Afro-Americans.**

The Army's racial affirmative action is geared de facto to blacks. This principle should be generalized throughout our society. The basic social dichotomy in our society is black versus white and, increasingly, black versus nonblack. The core reality is that blacks have a dual sense of identity and grievance with America, one that is unique and far stronger than any other ethnic group's sense of belonging or not belonging. The confluence of race, slavery, and segregation has created a social reality that in the American experience is unparalleled. (Perhaps the Native American Indian story comes closest.) Multiculturalism ultimately trivializes the distinct history and predicament of black Americans. The Afro-American story is singular and of such magnitude that it cannot be compared to the experiences of other American ethnic groups, especially immigrant groups.[37] American blacks resemble neither the immigrants of yesterday nor the ones of today.

Likewise, affirmative action based on class or income is a chimera.[38] Not only is it much more difficult to implement than affirmative action based on race, ethnicity, or gender, but the nonblack poor would soon displace blacks in affirmative action procedures. More to the point, we argue that race overrides class as a source of ingrained prejudice in our country. (Ask yourself: Would the child of a white ditchdigger or that of a black physician cause more strain by marrying into a white family?) Affirmative action based on class or income, paradoxically, would work against black Americans, the very group for which it is most justified. Afro-Americans already are increasingly apprehensive that the "wide net" approach to affirmative action is another way of excluding blacks from channels of opportunity. A policy of class-based affirmative action would confirm these apprehensions.

Terminology on affirmative action is instructive. When the issue was defined originally as focusing on Afro-Americans, the preferred term was "equal opportunity." "Multiculturalism" and "diversity" as affirmative action concepts entered the vocabulary only after nonblack groups came to be included in the programs. The decline of Afro-Americans in affirmative action priorities corresponded directly with replacement of equal opportunity with the rhetoric of multiculturalism and diversity.

⬛★ *Lesson Ten:* **Recognize Afro-Anglo Culture as the Core American Culture.**

American history needs a reconstruction to stress how much our nation's culture and moral vision derive from the Afro-American experience. White Americans must recognize the Afro-American elements in our bedrock culture; equally, black Americans must recognize their contributions to the common American culture and resist the lure of an Afrocentric curriculum that too easily obscures the contribution of Afro-Americans to our national heritage. In black thought, a duality persists on whether blacks are essentially outsiders with strong African connections or are quintessential Americans.[39] To the question, "Are blacks Americans?" the Army experience offers a resounding "Yes." This also means, in the sense of shared culture, that "Americans are part black." This may be the only way to lance the boil of a black "oppositional" culture. Just as we came to recognize our shared American religious culture as Judeo-Christian in origin, we hope for an acknowledgment of our common Afro-Anglo heritage.

We must abandon the mindset that being "black" and being "American" are mutually exclusive. This is a false dichotomy, though held by many black nationalists and most whites. Being black and being American is not an "either-or" dichotomy but a "both-and" relationship. The titles of the only two autobiographies by black generals are informative: *American* by Benjamin O. Davis, Jr., and *My American Journey* by Colin L. Powell.[40]

★★ *Lesson Eleven:* **Enhancing Black Participation Is Good for Organizational Effectiveness.**

The blunt truth is that the way most Americans see it, the greater the black proportion in an organization, the poorer its effectiveness. The armed forces (along with historically black educational institutions) are the welcome exceptions. Two plain facts have profound meaning: first, the disproportionately black Army stands out as one of the most respected organizations in American society; and second, General Colin L. Powell occupies the pinnacle of American esteem. Not only has the military played a central role as an avenue of black achievement but it has also shown that a large Afro-American presence has been conducive to the smooth operation of a major American institution.

Indeed, the increase in the proportion of blacks has corresponded with an increase in the standing and effectiveness of the Army. Other variables also contributed to this improved state of affairs, but the military's early implementation of affirmative action and its enhancement of black achievement were necessary preconditions. Ultimately, any race-relations program must pass a single test. In the not-so-long run, does it improve organizational performance?

★★ *Lesson Twelve:* **If We Do Not Overcome Race, American Society May Unravel.**

The final lesson of the Army experience is political. A society no longer united by foreign threats may discover that its own internal racial divisions are deeper and more intractable than anyone realized. The growing centrifugal tensions in America could easily make national unity the issue of the twenty-first century.

The military of the 1970s recognized that its race problem was so critical that it was on the verge of self-destruction. That realization set in motion the steps that have led to today's relatively positive state of affairs. As racial division grows in American society at large, will we come to the same realization?

Appendix
National Service:
The Civic Equivalent
of the Draft

The armed forces are shrinking at a rapid rate since the end of the Cold War. Active-duty strength has fallen from 2.1 million in the late 1980s to 1.5 million in 1995. While the proportion of blacks in the military has remained constant during that period, the drawdown has resulted in an actual decline in the number of Afro-Americans in uniform, from 450,000 in 1989 to 300,000 in 1995.[1] Barring unforeseen global developments, the number of Americans serving in the armed forces is programmed to drop to 1.2 million by the end of the decade, and some observers say even this figure is unrealistically high.

While the post–Cold War military drawdown has received much attention, we must not forget that an equally large reduction in forces accompanied the end of the Vietnam era. During the peacetime draft years between the wars in Korea and Vietnam, active-duty military strength stood at about 2.5 million, surpassing the number that are now serving by more than a million. During these peacetime draft years, close to 40 percent of all black males reaching age 18 served in the armed forces, a figure that remained about the same during the Vietnam era. After the end of the Vietnam War and the draft in 1973, the proportion declined to 15 percent. With the end of the Cold War and the accompanying drawdown, the proportion of black men entering the military in 1995 has fallen to 8 percent.

Thus we must seek approaches that would fill a national need, would provide obvious benefits for the country as a whole, and by virtue of organization and policies, would provide most of the racial benefits now furnished by the armed forces. A comprehensive national service program for youth is the only way to achieve all these goals.

National Service and Civic Content

A major philosophical obstacle stands in the way of building a national service program on the scale of the armed forces: most observers see the military and the civilian as somehow in opposition to each other. People are used to thinking of military and civilian service as alternative ideals and even opposing character types: the tough-minded and the high-minded. We strongly disagree with that assumption. The division is more apparent than real, once we recognize that citizen duty must underlie any form of national service.

The idea of national service is conventionally traced to William James's 1910 essay "The Moral Equivalent of War."[2] James sought to contrast the noble qualities evoked by war—"intrepidity, contempt for softness, surrender of private interest, obedience to command"—with the destructive purposes they served. Is it not possible, he asked, to call forth the same heroism without the shooting and the bloodshed? National service, he answered, presented a means by which a democratic nation could maintain social cohesion without having to go to war.

James's essay set the tone of discussion for decades to come. In retrospect, however, it is unclear whether James's effort was an important beginning or an unfortunate detour. Although he consciously tried to steer a middle road between what he termed the "war-party" and the "peace-party," James was nonetheless an avowed pacifist and almost instinctively described civilian service as clearly superior to military service.[3] For this reason, neo-Jamesians continue to portray civilian duty as the most noble form of national service, with a consequent belittlement (if not hatred) of military service. How else could Robert Coles, the eminent psychiatrist at Harvard University and a veteran, write a book entitled *The Call of Service* (1993), which makes only passing reference to military service while lauding many types of civilian service?[4]

Contrary to James and his followers, the virtue of military service rests not in its martial values but in its character, in a democratic society, as one of the deepest forms of citizenship obligation. National service involves the performance of citizen duties that give individuals a sense of the civic whole, a whole that is more important than any single person or group of persons. This is the hallmark of military service. The same is true of civilian service as well. The idea of national service builds on the same sense of fulfillment of civic obligation, some sense of participation in a public life with other citizens. Hereafter, we will refer to these notions as *civic content*.

Military and civilian service, if not quite a seamless garment, are, insofar as they both contain civic content, cut from the same cloth. The citizen-soldier is both a unique type and an archetype for national service. Instead of shying away from the military analogy, supporters of civilian national service must respond to the shared civic content. To the degree proponents of civilian service recognize this, national service can recapitulate the racial success story of the armed forces.

Many national service supporters also are confused about who is supposed to benefit from the work performed: the server or society. The result is two schools of thought about national service, which might be called the *instrumental* and the *civic*. The instrumental tradition justifies national service by the good done for the server; the civic tradition focuses on the value of the services performed. The first tradition provokes negative stereotypes by inviting speculation on deficiencies in the character of the server. The second tradition offers national service as an end in itself, thereby fostering positive images of servers.

One other issue must be gotten out of the way early on. Because civic content is the lodestone of national service, whether the service performed is compulsory or voluntary is not an essential element of the definition of national service, however profound the policy implications of that question may be. We will propose a comprehensive national service that would include a substantial number of youth—as many as one million—in either military or civilian service; this service would not be mandatory. A program of such size could become the functional equivalent of the conscription in terms of youth serving and receiving educational benefits correspondent with GI Bill educational benefits granted military veterans.

A civically oriented national service program must rest ultimately on enlightened patriotism.[5] The critical step in making the case for such a patriotism is not so much to grasp why those in power deserve to be distrusted (seldom a difficult task) but to see that power can be fashioned so that it deserves trust and loyalty. There is no reason to be ashamed of a patriotism that reminds us of the enduring worth of America's civic institutions, even if many were long excluded from their benefits and others still do not have their fair share. Enlightened patriotism involves reason and criticism as well as emotional ties to the nation-state. Such self-critical patriotism is quite different from one that amounts to enthusiastic acceptance of the status quo. Patriotism, like other human virtues, must be tempered by balance and reflection. But it is patriotism that underlies military service and so it must be for civilian service.

The supporters of civilian and military service have more in common than they realize. Both parties agree that national service must stand apart from marketplace considerations. Both call for participation by a large cross section of American youth. The central point is that even though national service comes in many shapes and sizes, the unity of civic content is of more lasting consequence than the diversity of civilian and military.

National Youth Service: From the 1930s Through the 1980s

The precursors of national youth service can be traced to the nineteenth century, but it took the Great Depression of the 1930s to place it on center stage.[6] Two of the most successful initiatives of the New Deal were national service programs: the Civilian Conservation Corps and the National Youth Administration.

The better known of the two, the Civilian Conservation Corps (CCC), was primarily rural in emphasis. The idea of the CCC originated with Franklin Delano Roosevelt himself who, as governor of New York, initiated a state reforestation program for unemployed young men. Within two years of the CCC's creation in 1933, some 1,500 camps were located in all parts of the nation, but mainly on public lands in the western states. The work varied with the location, but the main projects were soil conservation, tree planting, flood control, trail-blazing, and road building. The camps drew on the services of numerous government agencies. The Army administered the camps and was responsible for all aspects of CCC life except the work projects themselves, which were managed mainly by the Department of the Interior and the Forest Service. Recruitment was handled by the Labor Department.

In the original design (which changed slightly over the years), enrollees were unemployed single males 18 to 25 years of age with no criminal record. Enrollment lasted six months and was renewable up to two years. Participants received food, shelter, uniforms, and a monthly payment of $30, two-thirds of it sent directly to the enrollee's family. Enrollment peaked during the mid-1930s at 500,000 a year. By the time the program ended in 1942, nearly 3 million young men had participated.

The CCC was no shining example of equal opportunity. CCC camps were strictly segregated and only eight in a hundred CCC members were Afro-American, a figure well below the proportion of blacks among young unemployed males.

Although the CCC enjoyed widespread popularity, it was not without problems. Unions feared that the subsistence pay of the program would drive down wages. About one enrollee in four deserted or received an administrative discharge. The Army's role, moreover, promoted concern that the CCC was being used to "militarize" youth. Yet only on the very eve of World War II were rudimentary military drills

NATIONAL SERVICE ★ 149

introduced in CCC camps, and the Army's involvement never became a real issue.

The National Youth Administration (NYA), a favorite project of Eleanor Roosevelt, was primarily an urban program, and it had a much better track record on racial matters. The NYA had a special Office of Negro Affairs, whose head, Mary McLeod Bethune, served as a liaison between the Roosevelt administration and the black community. The NYA did not discriminate against blacks, who made up about 15 percent of the enrollees, and resorted to segregation only in areas where doing otherwise would provoke violence. In contrast to the all-male CCC, about half the NYA volunteers were women, and they were coequal participants with the men.

Over the lifespan of the NYA, 1935–43, nearly five million young men and women participated. A typical stipend was $15 a month. Initially it recruited only individuals who were on relief, but later drew upon the merely unemployed, permitting a much wider recruiting pool. Activities included work training programs, education classes for unemployed youths, upgrading of public facilities, and filling jobs in government agencies. In a forerunner of what would later be called work-study programs, an estimated 12 percent of the nation's college students worked part-time for the NYA, the first time federal government aid had been offered to college students (excluding ROTC scholarships).

President Roosevelt gave some thought to putting national service on a more permanent footing. In 1940 he announced that he would recommend some form of compulsory service for all young men: either active-duty military service or civilian defense work. Roosevelt broached the topic of national service again in a 1943 news conference. Looking to the postwar future, he said he objected to the term "compulsory military service" and preferred to speak instead of a "year's contribution of service to the government."[7] In 1944, a year before his death, Roosevelt said the service he had in mind was closer to the CCC model than to military service. The president's fragmentary remarks never made clear exactly what he thought about the relationship between military and civilian service. Many years would pass before national service again received such high-level sponsorship.

The 1950s were the doldrums for the idea of civilian national service, but the climate changed with the presidency of John F. Kennedy. During his 1960 campaign, Kennedy advocated the creation of an overseas youth corps, and set up the Peace Corps shortly after his election. When the Peace Corps was established, Third World people had seen few Americans who were not religious missionaries, soldiers, or affluent tourists. Peace Corps volunteers showed the world a different kind of American: one who spoke the local language and lived under local conditions. It also showed that thousands of young Americans had enough of an adventurous spirit to go into strange lands and perform services that Americans had rarely attempted before. In 1966, the peak year, the Peace Corps employed some 15,000 young people.

For all its achievements, the Peace Corps has had a stormy history. After the heady years of the Kennedy administration, the corps entered a period of decline as it became defensive about its reputation as a draft evaders' haven during the Vietnam era. Membership in the Peace Corps, however, never gave a statutory exemption from conscription; local draft boards decided how to deal with Peace Corps volunteers. A few men were drafted out of the Peace Corps, but most were granted deferments; some were drafted after their Peace Corps stint.

Under Richard M. Nixon, the autonomy and visibility of the Peace Corps was sharply reduced. When Jimmy Carter took office, he appointed Sam Brown, a leading anti–Vietnam War organizer, to direct ACTION, the agency that oversaw the Peace Corps. This appointment only heightened the contrast between the images of the Peace Corps and the military. Under

Ronald Reagan, the Peace Corps attained some measure of equilibrium, though at a reduced level. At that time, the Peace Corps took another turn in a long-simmering debate. The "generalists," who favored recruiting untrained youths, were pitted against the "specialists," who believed in sending experienced volunteers to perform specific tasks. The new focus was reflected in the shifting age composition of the Peace Corps. In the peak year, 1966, almost nine out of ten volunteers were 26 years old or younger; fifteen years later, only four out of ten were. By the late 1980s, the pendulum began to swing back. During the 1990s, the proportion of young volunteers climbed back to half of all Peace Corps members.

Despite its many changes of fortune, the Peace Corps has proved remarkably durable. Since its inception, some 140,000 volunteers have served in 92 countries. In 1995 three-quarters of the 6,800 Peace Corps volunteers were under the age of 30. Afro-Americans accounted for only 2.8 percent of all the volunteers (but 4 percent of those serving in Africa). With a 1995 budget of $231 million, the average costs came to about $33,000 for each volunteer.

The early success of the Peace Corps made a domestic equivalent seem a natural sequel. In 1964, VISTA (Volunteers in Service to America) was formed as part of President Lyndon B. Johnson's Great Society program. The early VISTA was patterned after the Peace Corps: some 2,000 volunteers were given assignments away from their homes following six months of training. Participants received a subsistence allowance and free health insurance. The VISTA organization made federal grants to sponsoring agencies— local government offices and nonprofit associations—which hired the VISTA volunteers and oversaw their activities, mainly in urban slums and depressed rural areas.

In 1969 Congress authorized the recruitment of low-income individuals to do VISTA work in their home communities, and enrollment rose through the 1970s to a peak of

5,000 in 1980. During the Carter years, VISTA became embroiled in controversy when given the responsibility of "empowering the poor," which soon led to volunteer-organized tenant strikes and welfare-rights advocacy. This, as well as certain VISTA grants to organizations with strong New Left ties, antagonized some moderate and conservative members of Congress. More significant, however, was the change in the social demographics of VISTA. From an original recruitment base of affluent white youths, VISTA came to enlist people who were primarily poor and over the age of 35. In the early cohorts, blacks accounted for only one VISTA member in twenty; by 1970, the ratio was one in three, where it has remained.

When the Reagan administration began its first term, it set out to do away with what it viewed as a leftist bastion. VISTA survived, but what remained was barely recognizable. Membership was cut to about 2,000 volunteers (only 400 under age 26). A pro forma "orientation" session by the sponsoring agencies replaced the common training period of the early years. Even worse, VISTA did not recruit on college campuses after 1980. For all practical purposes, it ceased to exist as a national youth-recruiting program during the Reagan and Bush administrations. A young person seeking national service would have found it difficult, if not impossible, to enter a federal youth service program. In 1992 fewer than 2,500 young people were in the Peace Corps and VISTA combined. Matters changed with the Clinton administration; in 1995, Peace Corps and VISTA enrollment combined exceeded 10,000 members.

Service was the initial impetus for both Peace Corps and VISTA. In their early years, they far surpassed earlier civilian youth programs in their level of civic content. Starting with Lyndon Johnson's administration but especially in Richard Nixon's, emphasis shifted away from notions of broadly based national service toward employment programs targeted at poor and minority youth. Programs such as the Job Corps (founded in 1964), the Neighborhood Youth Corps (1965–73), the Comprehensive Employment and Training Act (1973–83), and the Job Training Partnership Act (1983 to the present) were devoid of any civic content; instead, they were job or job-training programs. Because most of these federal programs were targeted at disadvantaged young people, any cross section of American youth was precluded.

What might have seemed like the nadir of national service at the federal level was belied by developments at the state and local levels. By 1993, 74 "year-round" and 15 "seasonal" programs existed, with a membership of 23,000.[8] The year-round youth corps varied widely, but they belonged to three broad groups: state conservation corps, county and city programs, and social service programs. Most of these became part of an umbrella organization, the National Association of Service and Conservation Corps (NASCC). Black participation was high, accounting for 28 percent of the corps' participants.

Paralleling and promoting the revived interest in youth corps at state and local levels, other volunteer youth service programs blossomed in the 1980s and continued into the 1990s. The Campus Outreach Opportunity League (COOL) enlisted tens of thousands of students to serve on more than 800 campuses. YouthBuild, a network for training low-income minority participants to help rebuild houses in their own neighborhoods, was established a year later.

City Year in Boston has become a model of a mixed-class, mixed-race local corps.[9] A vignette contrasts how the races get along in the Army and in a local corps when facing a common source of contention: what music to listen to. Most City Year work sites have a "boom box" to which all the volunteers at the site listen, Steven Waldman recounts. Inner-city blacks prefer rap while white suburban youth prefer rock.

They compromised by listening to "oldies" from the 1960s and 1970s, music liked by neither group but inoffensive to both. In similar situations in today's Army, certain music is off limits in mixed racial settings: "gansta rap" for whites and "heavy metal" for blacks. Whites and blacks each can veto what they consider offensive music. The Army compromise—taking turns playing mainstream rap and mainstream rock—allows both white and black soldiers to have a turn at listening to music with which they can connect.

The Revived Debate on National Service

Interest in youth service on the national level was revived in 1988, when the Democratic Leadership Council (DLC), an organization of forward-looking Democrats set up to counter the party's conventional left liberalism, proposed its own national service program. The following year, two prominent DLC leaders, Senator Sam Nunn of Georgia and Congressman Dave McCurdy of Oklahoma, introduced a bill based on the council's proposal. The Citizenship and National Service Act called for the establishment of a Citizen Corps of up to a million enrollees, who would serve one or two years in a civilian capacity, or two years in the military. In exchange, the participants would receive education vouchers worth $10,000 for a year of civilian service and $12,000 for a year of military service.[10] These vouchers could be used for vocational training, college, or graduate school. The conceptual breakthrough was the linkage of military and civilian service under the broader heading of national service. The policy breakthrough was the broadening of the GI Bill principle to include civilian as well as military service to the nation. Thus, the citizen soldier and the civilian server were linked in a single proposal, ending the historical philosophical polarization between military and civilian service.

The political reaction to the Nunn-McCurdy Bill was instructive. Predictably, the libertarian right opposed the bill, mainly because of its opposition to any form of federal student aid. Milton Friedman, the Nobel laureate economist, and Martin Anderson, President Reagan's chief domestic adviser, were particularly prominent on this side of the debate. More surprising was the vociferous opposition of the higher education establishment and its liberal allies on Capitol Hill. The attack by the education establishment was based on deep-seated antipathy to a service-based criterion for eligibility to receive federal student aid. Indeed, when the GI Bill lapsed after the Vietnam War and was reintroduced in 1985 by Congressman G. V. (Sonny) Montgomery (D-Miss.), the university community was not visible in either lamenting its end or supporting its resurrection. Thus the National Service Act came into conflict not only with the "every man for himself" philosophy of the conservative right but also with the "something for nothing" philosophy of the liberal left.

Opponents of the Nunn-McCurdy Bill argued that linking federal aid to service would entice only poor and predominantly black students into national service. These defenders of the status quo conveniently overlooked the regressive nature of the present system: only slightly more than half of all high school graduates go on to college (one third of blacks), and about half of these graduate with a bachelor's degree (one third of blacks). By greatly expanding opportunities to enter youth corps, the Nunn-McCurdy Bill, in the manner of the original GI Bill, would have offered new options for college or vocational training to many youths who would otherwise lack such a chance.

Although the Nunn-McCurdy Bill did not move far in Congress, it set the stage for the National and Community Service Act, a more modest initiative by three other Democrats, Senators Barbara A. Mikulski of Maryland, Edward M.

Kennedy of Massachusetts, and Harris Wofford of Pennsylvania. In 1990 they called for the creation of a commission to fund and evaluate local public service efforts that might serve as models for larger programs and to raise the public consciousness about the benefits and issues surrounding national service. To the surprise of many, because national service was essentially a Democratic initiative, President Bush signed the legislation in November 1990. The reason was simple: the backers of the National and Community Service Act had included in the bill funding for President Bush's own pet program: the Points of Light Foundation, which sought to encourage volunteerism in nonprofit organizations.

The new law authorized creation of a Commission on National and Community Service, governed by a bipartisan board of directors. During its two-year existence, the commission awarded grants to local youth corps, community organizations, primary and secondary schools, and colleges. The commission was a paragon of efficiency: it gave out $75 million annually with a staff of only twenty. (By contrast, the Points of Light Foundation during its first years of operation granted $4 million to service organizations while spending $22 million on promotions and administrative expenses.)[11]

A reading of the commission's 1993 report—*What You Can Do for Your Country*—did, however, contain some troubling aspects. The report described youth corps "at their best" to be those that "encourage a service ethic, help corps members develop job skills and discipline, and create a sense of community."[12] Notably absent or given low priority was what of value the national servers would do for the country. Thomas Ehrlich, as chairman of the commission, went so far as to state: "We focus on the individual—self-esteem, confidence, character."[13] The commission, moreover, explicitly opposed large federal programs such as the Civilian Conservation Corps. It favored support of preexisting service organizations and efforts to create new ones at the local level. Competition

NATIONAL SERVICE ★ 157

among local service organizations for volunteers and funds could stimulate innovation. In fact, however, two years and $150 million later, few Americans had much idea of what had been accomplished in the way of national service.

A special convocation of youths who had worked in a Summer of Service was scheduled in San Francisco at the end of summer 1993 to highlight the new spirit of national service. Some 1,500 young people from around the country took part in the program; fewer than a third of the participants were white.[14] Instead of being a showcase session, the meeting almost turned into a fiasco. It showed the pitfalls of youth service programs that lose sight of the military analogy. The participants soon split into black, Hispanic, Native American, and gay/lesbian caucuses. Students harangued the White House organizers about the need to organize poor people to demand benefits and about the gay ban in the military.[15] Fortunately, the balkanization of the youth servers received little press coverage. If coverage had been fuller, the national service bill might not have passed a month later. Even so, the polarity between military and civilian service could hardly have been drawn more sharply.

AmeriCorps

During the 1992 presidential campaign, Bill Clinton made national service one of his key campaign planks, part of the "New Democrat" image he projected from his DLC background. Once in office, he placed national service among his top priorities. In September 1993, the president signed a slimmed-down version of his national service proposal, the National and Community Service Trust Act of 1993. The act had the broad support of Democratic congressional members from Senator Sam Nunn to Senator Edward Kennedy as well as backing from many moderate Republicans.

The act set up a Corporation for National and Community Service (which superseded the commission set up two years earlier) to oversee the management and funding of what was soon named the AmeriCorps program. The first head of the corporation was Eli J. Segal, a longtime Clinton associate and successful Boston businessman. Although he entered the position with neither a military nor a civilian service background, Segal proved himself a skilled tactician in negotiating the passage of the bill and, later, an effective executive of the corporation.

The act provided $1.5 billion for fiscal years 1994, 1995, and 1996 to fund 100,000 AmeriCorps participants. Two-thirds of the funds would be funneled through bipartisan state commissions, which would disburse the funds to local agencies and nonprofit organizations. All grants would, however, be screened and approved by the corporation. To spur innovation, AmeriCorps would create national competition among programs. Enrollees would work in nonprofit agencies, community centers, parks, government agencies, and public hospitals. Tasks were categorized into four major groups: education, public safety, human services, and environmental services. During 1994, in the first round of grant money, $300 million was disbursed to 350 programs at more than 700 sites—a diffuse distribution.

Although AmeriCorps emphasized local programs, it also included two that were operated nationally. One was a beefed-up VISTA. The other, entirely new and more expansive, was the National Civilian Community Corps (NCCC). The NCCC was modeled after the old Civilian Conservation Corps, but on a much smaller scale, with only about 1,000 members in 1995. After a four-week orientation course on one of four "campuses," former military bases, NCCC enrollees performed eleven months of service in various parts of the country. The NCCC was the only AmeriCorps program that had any common training experience.

Significantly, the black occupying the highest leadership position in AmeriCorps, Donald L. Scott, was a retired Army brigadier general. Scott was vice president of the Corporation for National and Community Service and the first head of the NCCC. Scott was an ROTC graduate of Lincoln College, a historically black college in Missouri.

We spent a day in Washington, D.C., observing and talking with NCCC teams at work. Twenty-four young people were doing rehabilitation work in the Arthur Capper Senior Apartments located in an impoverished neighborhood in the capital's southeast quadrant. The teams had female majorities, were about a quarter black, and most members had some college (though rarely degrees). The teams had come to Washington, D.C., from their home bases in Maryland and South Carolina (while in Washington they resided in a nearby youth hostel). After a day's training on painting, caulking, tile laying, and fumigating, the NCCC teams quickly went to work fixing up a dilapidated apartment in the housing project.

The Capper Apartments, a federally funded facility, was originally set up as a senior citizen home, but in recent years, much to the dismay of the older residents (virtually all of them black), had been forced to take in younger homeless and mentally disturbed individuals. The "Resident President," a veteran of four years' service during the Korean War era, said of the youths: "They are a godsend. Everybody wants AmeriCorps. We just wish there were more of them. We'd have to wait forever for HUD [Housing and Urban Development] to get the job done. Without these kids this place would be a ruin."

When the job first started the NCCC youths were introduced to the residents at a communal meeting. Except for a few newer arrivals, the residents were extremely receptive, and their attitude was greatly appreciated by the team members. One of the formerly homeless tenants admonished a black team member: "Why are you working so hard? You should put that [paint] brush in a white boy's hands." She responded: "That's the attitude that got you into the mess you're in. You ought to be ashamed of yourself."

Asked about their reasons for joining AmeriCorps, the team members gave varied responses, but certain themes were recurrent. They wanted to do something different, serve a good cause, get away from home—and they liked the idea of working with people from different backgrounds. The educational benefits following service were also very attractive to them.

Many of these motives echo those given by armed forces recruits. Indeed, virtually every team member had thought seriously about joining the military. Why had they opted for AmeriCorps instead? The overriding reason was that they saw the stereotype of excessive military discipline as unsuited to their own dispositions. One young white woman, just out of high school, gave an insightful answer. "NCCC is kind of in-between the Army and going straight to college or getting a regular job. We want to serve our country. We are a team. We wear a uniform. We get help to go to college. We get to meet all kinds of people. But we are not bossed around the way you are in the Army. We have our freedom."

The Politics of National Service

AmeriCorps participants had to be age 17 or older and high school graduates, or agree to earn a general equivalency diploma. Enrollees would be chosen without discrimination, although special attention would be given to disadvantaged youths. The basic term of service would be one or two years of full-time duty. Options for two or three years of part-time service would also be available in some cases. Enrollees would be paid 85 percent of the minimum wage, coming to around $7,400 annually, plus health insurance. Full-time participants could also receive child care, if necessary.

A key provision of the bill gave educational grants to enrollees. For each year of service, a participant would receive an educational voucher worth $4,725, to be used for vocational education, college, or graduate school or to pay off a college loan. Thus, for two years of service, the maximum grant would be $9,450. This contrasts with the $20,000 educational benefit that would have been given a two-year civilian server under the original Nunn-McCurdy Bill. Still, when all is said and done, the 1993 act set a notable precedent. The principle of linking federal educational aid to some form of civilian service—a small but still recognizable civilian variant of the GI Bill—was codified into law.

The amount of the educational benefit was a subject of much haggling, and its final determination deserves comment. The Clinton administration initially wanted to offer a $7,500 educational benefit for each year of service, but this raised the ire of two groups: the Department of Defense and veterans' organizations. The armed forces were concerned that a generous civilian postservice educational benefit would siphon off possible military recruits; the veterans disliked the suggestion that civilian service was worthy of the same rewards as military service. The Clinton administration, still sensitive about controversies over the president's lack of military service and his initiative on gays in the military, did not want to fight these groups. It agreed to an educational benefit for civilian service equal to 80 percent of the minimum postservice educational benefit that a member of the military can earn.

In fact, the compensation available to a civilian server under AmeriCorps did not come close to what someone in the military might earn. An Army private receives a basic compensation of $17,000 a year, well over twice an Ameri-

Corps member's stipend. This does not include enlistment bonuses. Many recruits, moreover, are eligible for added Army educational bonuses that double the basic GI Bill entitlement. For example, a high school graduate who scores in the top half of the test distribution and serves in the combat arms can receive more than $28,000 in educational benefits after two years of military service. That amounts to about $18,000 more than civilian service earnings.

Moreover, the Pentagon's concern about losing out on recruits now appears unfounded. Studies by the Army Recruiting Command show that military recruitment would have been helped, not hurt, by the original Nunn-McCurdy proposal.[16] It seems that making some form of national service a prerequisite for federal college aid would have caused more young Americans to opt for military service than do now, even though many would choose civilian service instead.

If the negotiations on the educational benefit perhaps showed an oversensitivity to the military, the Corporation for National and Community Service displayed a characteristic blind spot toward military service in another way. Under the corporation's direction, each state set up a twenty-five-person national service commission. Fourteen of these positions were earmarked for members of special categories: young people, senior citizens, public school officials, local government, labor, business, community action agencies, and persons with "service-learning experience." All this and more, not to mention diversity in terms of race, ethnicity, and sex—yet not one of these specified categories included military experience.

President Clinton stated that AmeriCorps was one of his proudest accomplishments. Setting up a national service program from a standing start was indeed a tremendous achievement. Little surprise, then, when the Republicans, the new congressional majority in 1994, immediately placed AmeriCorps on the budgetary chopping block. Speaker of the

House Newt Gingrich said he was "totally, unequivocally opposed to national service." He lambasted AmeriCorps as "coerced volunteerism."[17]

The Republican speaker's hostility to national service also had an upside. The time had come to refocus public attention on the philosophy and program of national service. For starters, let us clarify the terminology. AmeriCorps members are not "volunteers" inasmuch as they receive a modest stipend and education benefit. AmeriCorps participants should be called corps members, servers, or enrollees. Gingrich's designation of "coerced volunteerism" is an oxymoron that misses the point. Do we object when we call our military an "all-volunteer force" even though soldiers earn a decent salary? Or that a member of the Peace Corps is officially called a "Peace Corps volunteer" even when paid a stipend equivalent to that of an AmeriCorps server?

AmeriCorps faces a core paradox. Set up to be run mainly through local agencies and nonprofit organizations, AmeriCorps seemingly was in tune with the trend toward local control and decentralization. But only youth service programs that are federally run and centralized organizations have credibility and name recognition. The blunt fact is that only one in four Americans had even heard of AmeriCorps during its first years of operation and even fewer knew what it was doing. Remarkably, even among young Americans, ages 18 to 24, more could identify the Civilian Conservation Corps (28 percent) of the Depression era than the contemporary AmeriCorps (24 percent).[18] National service is, after all, national.

AmeriCorps also tends to get mushy—or, as Gingrich put it, "gimmicky." Proponents of AmeriCorps too often stress how community service benefits the young person, instead of what the server actually does. Young people doing calisthenics in youth corps T-shirts is not the way to build a constituency for national service.

Another trouble spot must be pointed out: a skewed political base. Support for youth corps should by no means be seen as a program for political liberals. After all, it was the centrist Democratic Leadership Council that initiated the contemporary move to national service. Conservative icon William F. Buckley, Jr., long an exponent of civic duty, has been an eloquent advocate of the cause.[19] James J. Pinkerton, a key policy adviser in the Bush administration, has made a strong case for the Civilian Conservation Corps.[20] Liberal proponents of AmeriCorps must practice diversity when they seek counsel on national service. Bipartisan input is a prerequisite of bipartisan support. The lack of such support placed AmeriCorps on the budget chopping block in 1995 and put its very existence into question.[21]

A 1995 Gallup Poll allows for some comparisons by race on attitudes toward national service. Almost identical numbers, 79 percent of blacks and 81 percent of whites, believed it is an excellent or good idea for a young person to spend one year in national service.[22] When young people were asked whether they would personally serve in a national service program, however, the results differed markedly by race. Black youth were twice as likely (57 percent) as white youth (28 percent) to say they were very much or somewhat interested in joining a program like AmeriCorps.[23]

According to the same Gallup Poll, 41 percent of a national sample favor limiting federal student aid only to those college students who have served their country in either a military or a civilian capacity. This is a striking level of support for a policy that has not even been articulated on the national stage. Indeed, the GI Bill aspect could well become the main appeal of national service to the American public.

In 1995 Harris Wofford, the former senator from Pennsylvania, succeeded Eli Segal as head of the National Service Corporation (the shortened name of the corporation since

1994). Wofford had been a longtime proponent of national service and was one of the original sponsors of the legislation in the Senate. Wofford brought unusual credentials to the position: He had served in the Army during World War II, been a college president, was active in civil rights, and had been instrumental in setting up the Peace Corps during the Kennedy administration. While still in the Senate in 1992, Wofford had successfully introduced legislation to commemorate Martin Luther King Day as a day of service. Upon assuming his responsibilities at AmeriCorps, Wofford indicated that the time had come to rethink national service as well as outreach to a broader political base. The direction would most likely be toward greater federal expansion of education benefits for youth servers and more local involvement on funding the stipends received by servers. Whether these initiatives have come soon enough, only time will tell, but the new thinking at AmeriCorps augurs well for the future of AmeriCorps, if there is to be one.

Military Service as the Model for Civilian Service

We have gone into some detail in recapitulating the history of national service in America because we consider it the main alternative to military service for overcoming race in our society. While AmeriCorps was squarely in the civilian tradition of national service, perhaps too much so, the 1990s also saw a growing tendency to use the military more directly in youth training and education. Some of this trend was due to the demand to find new avenues of employment for active-duty members and those separated or retired from the military in the wake of the post-Soviet military drawdown.[24] Another factor was the premise that military personnel have special strengths—black representation, a predominantly male makeup, and mentoring skills—that could make them effective teachers and role models. There was also a growing belief that the military structure in itself could help straighten out wayward youth.[25]

One ambitious National Guard project is the "Youth Challenge Program," a remediation program for at-risk youths.[26] In 1993 the National Guard began to establish camps in fifteen states based on a rigorous military regime (not to be confused with more than fifty state-run or local boot-camp prisons across the country). These boot-camp educational programs help high school dropouts earn general equivalency degrees or diplomas. Youth Challenge offers a five-month residential program and a year-long follow-up mentoring program. The students live in barracks, are awakened at 5:30 A.M., and undergo physical training as well as seven hours of classroom study each weekday. To be eligible, an enrollee must be unemployed and not involved with drugs or the criminal justice system. The structured environment is designed to instill a sense of discipline in the students' lives. An enrollee who completes the program receives a stipend of $2,200.

This effort does not come cheaply. In June 1993 President Clinton signed a $44 million appropriation, including start-up costs, to train 2,500 teenage youths. Once up and running, the program will cost an estimated $12,000 a year per youth. Early results were encouraging, but not across the board. The first Youth Challenge program to open, in Connecticut, was shut down in less than a year because of gang fighting among its enrollees.[27] About half of all who enter Youth Challenge leave with a diploma.

The "boot-camp" model in youth programs is not really a military analogy because it does not contain civic content. National service does not mean replicating the formal military structure or even using present or former members of the military. Instead, we look to the military model because it is the civic paradigm of national service. The differences between the tough-minded and the high-minded approaches

to national service are resolvable and even mutually rein-
forcing, once the two are joined under the banner of civic
duty. Otherwise the different concepts of military service
and civilian service will act like repelling magnets, pushing
away from each other.

Three main lessons can be derived by applying the military analogy to these experiences: national visibility counts,
definition and credibility matter, and the value of a service
to a community is paramount.

For visibility and recognition, local control and decentralization are not always a virtue. The armed forces are the
supreme example of a national, centralized institution with
high national visibility. Because AmeriCorps was so consciously decentralized, it was not highly visible nationally.
Although AmeriCorps' first-year membership of 20,000 was
greater than that of the Peace Corps at any time, AmeriCorps
did not approach the national recognition of the Peace
Corps. Even more striking, the glow of the highly centralized
and Army-run CCC remains strong in the national consciousness a half-century after its demise, while its decentralized and fully civilian counterpart, the NYA, is all but
forgotten.

Concerning the second reality, that definition speeds public comprehension and appreciation, AmeriCorps operates
under a severe handicap. Because civilian service is less
clearly defined than military service, it will probably have
less credibility in the larger society. AmeriCorps' functions—education, public safety, environment, neighborhood
development, and human needs—are too diffuse for easy
public comprehension of the national service mission.[28] This
need not be the case. In Germany some 100,000 young men,
conscientious objectors performing alternative service, have
become essential in keeping elderly people living in their
own homes by delivering meals-on-wheels, shopping for
groceries, and providing transportation to shopping and

medical facilities. The cost savings when elderly people live in their own homes, rather than in institutions, are tremendous. Significantly, since the early 1980s the German public has come to value civilian servers on a par with military draftees.[29] Indeed, in a supreme irony, the usefulness of civilian servers in Germany is now cited as an argument to maintain conscription!

A similar program assisting the elderly and disabled in the United States would feature both local control and high visibility—an expanded Capper House project on a national scale. Such an arrangement, in conjunction with a large federal conservation corps, would give national service the public recognition that has eluded it so far. The effectiveness of a national service policy can be assessed by asking a simple question: If the young server disappeared, would he or she be missed?

Concerning the third major principle, any civilian national service program must emulate the military, emphasizing the value of the service performed, not the presumed good for the server. The positive, but necessarily derivative, benefits of national service for the server can be achieved only when national service is cast in terms of civic content. After all, we do not have a military to help young men and women mature. The military performs this function well precisely because it is not defined as a remedial or welfare organization. For example, when Franklin Delano Roosevelt introduced the CCC, he stressed the concrete work that would be accomplished, not the self-improvement of the corps members. Such civic content is especially important if national service is to replicate the military's positive race relations.

Another important guidepost provided by the military relates to the social demographics of service programs. Whereas civilian national service programs have tended to be homogeneous by race and class—the upper-middle-class white Peace Corps, the poor minority youth corps—the armed forces in modern times have represented a much broader spectrum of American society. The hallmark of the contemporary military is a mixture of classes, regions, and races, though it is less complete than when conscription was in effect.

We must draw one final military analogy for national service. Military service is premised on a sense of duty, on the assumption that the common good is more important than individual rights, that the welfare of the whole supersedes individual rights. This need not be taken to military extremes in civilian national service, but it does correspond with ascendant communitarian thought that citizens have responsibilities as well as rights.[30]

We have asked many blacks in the Army what made a military career attractive to them as an avenue of mobility. Many replied that there were enough blacks in the Army to promise a certain degree of social comfort and professional support. Equally important, there were enough nonblacks and nonpoor people to prevent the Army from being perceived as a "black" institution or a haven for society's underclass. The Army, in short, delivered the uplift but not the stigma of a government social program. Any concept of national service for youths must recognize this.

The national service bill of 1993 crossed a major threshold, but it was handicapped by the lack of a military analogy. The general principle is clear: the more closely a civilian program can approach the substance, not necessarily the form, of the military model—federal and highly visible, oriented to service rather than the server, socially mixed, GI Bill–type benefits, and imbued with patriotism—the more successful it will be.

Notes

Preface

1. Charles Moskos, "Has the Army Killed Jim Crow?" *Negro History Bulletin*, vol. 21, no. 2 (May 1957), pp. 27–29; and John Sibley Butler, "Inequality in the Military: An Examination of Promotion Time for Black and White Enlisted Personnel," *American Sociological Review*, vol. 41 (October 1976), pp. 808–18.

2. John Sibley Butler, "Homosexuals and the Military Establishment," *Society* (November/December 1993), pp. 13–21.

3. For an extended critique of the term "African-American," see John Sibley Butler, "Multiple Identities," *Society* (May/June 1990), pp. 8–13. We are also greatly informed by Sterling Stuckey, "Identity and Ideology: The Names Controversy," in his *Slave Culture* (New York: Oxford University Press, 1987),

pp. 193–244; and John Hope Franklin, "On the Evolution of Scholarship in Afro-American History," in his *Race and History: Selected Essays* (Baton Rouge: Louisiana State University Press, 1989), pp. 49–58.

4. Carter G. Woodson, *The Mis-Education of the Negro* ([1933], reprinted Trenton, N.J.: African Press, 1990), p. 192. The name of the publisher has a certain irony in that Woodson— "The Father of Negro History"—eschewed the term "African" to describe American blacks.

Chapter 1

1. Andrew Hacker, *Two Nations: Black and White, Separate, Hostile, Unequal* (New York: Charles Scribner's Sons, 1992). Hacker's account of race relations is much more pessimistic than the Kerner Report assessment a generation earlier. See National Advisory Commission on Civil Disorders, *Report of the National Advisory Commission on Civil Disorders* (New York: Bantam Books, 1968). An excellent compilation on the state of sociological knowledge of Afro-Americans is Gerald Jaynes and Robin N. Williams, Jr., eds., *A Common Destiny: Blacks and American Society* (Washington, D.C.: National Academy Press, 1989).

2. Even in areas of American life where blacks have visibly succeeded in large numbers, such as the entertainment industry and professional sports, these achievements have been narrow, limited to exceedingly talented people, and rarely reflected among the organizational leadership of these endeavors.

3. Reynolds Farley and William H. Frey, "Changes in the Segregation of Whites from Blacks during the 1980s," *American Sociological Review*, vol. 59 (February 1994), pp. 23–45. This study of residential segregation is based on the 1990 census.

4. William H. Frey and Jonathan Tilove, "Immigrants In, Native Whites Out," *New York Times Magazine* (August 20, 1995), pp. 26–27; "Many Seek Security in Private Communities," *New York Times* (September 3, 1995), pp. 1, 10. For a fuller treatment of the persisting, if not growing, separation of the races, see Douglas S. Massey and Nancy A. Denton, eds., *American Apartheid: Segregation and the Making of the Underclass* (Cambridge, Mass.: Harvard University Press, 1993).

5. "Inquiry by Army Focuses on Hate," *New York Times*

(December 12, 1995), p. 1; "Racial Climate Is Evaluated," *Army Times* (December 25, 1995), p. 3.

6. The data reported here are based on surveys conducted by the authors in 1993 and 1995 in American Army units in the United States and abroad. The sample was drawn to represent a cross section of Army units. Total number surveyed included 464 blacks and 1,235 whites.

7. Among those surveyed by the authors, 35 percent of black soldiers and 66 percent of white soldiers agree with the statement that in the Army "all races are treated pretty much equally." Sixty-one percent of blacks thought whites got better treatment and 30 percent of whites thought minorities received better treatment.

8. Westat, Inc., *The 1985 Army Experience Survey, Tabular Descriptions of Mid-Career Separatees*, vol. 1 (Alexandria, Va.: Army Research Institute for the Behavioral and Social Sciences, 1986), p. 64.

9. Janice H. Laurence, *The Military: Purveyors of Fine Skills and Comportment for a Few Good Men* (Philadelphia: National Center on the Educational Quality of the Workforce, University of Pennsylvania, 1994), p. 14.

10. House Armed Services Committee Staff Task Force on Equality of Treatment and Opportunity in the Armed Forces, "An Assessment of Racial Discrimination in the Military: A Global Perspective" (December 30, 1994). See also "Military Short of Victory in War on Bias," *Washington Post* (April 29, 1995), pp. 1, 10, 11. A more positive view, written at about the same time, is Steven A. Holmes, "Time and Money Producing Racial Harmony in the Military," *New York Times* (April 5, 1995), pp. 1, 14.

11. *Washington Post* (April 10, 1995), p. 1.

12. For a discussion of why the black attrition rate is lower than that of whites, see Andrew Moskos, "Black Exceptionalism: Making It in the Military," *Black Issues in Higher Education*, vol. 7, no. 4 (April 26, 1990), p. 76.

13. Martin Binkin and Mark J. Eitelberg with Alvin J. Schexnider and Marvin M. Smith, *Blacks and the Military* (Washington, D.C.: The Brookings Institution, 1982), pp. 62–83.

14. Joseph M. Rothberg, Paul T. Bartone, Harry C. Holloway, and David H. Marlowe, "Life and Death in the U.S. Army," *Journal of the American Medical Association*, vol. 265, no. 7 (November 7, 1990), pp. 2241–44.

15. "F.B.I. Says at Least 7 Agents Attended Gathering Displaying

Racist Paraphernalia," *New York Times* (July 19, 1995), p. C18; "Good Ol' Boys Roundup Video Genuine," *Washington Times* (December 7, 1995), p. A4.

16. Ellis Cose, *The Rage of a Privileged Class* (New York: Harper-Collins, 1993). The manner in which race persists in defining relations within middle-class and professional circles has a growing, if recent, literature. See also Derrick Bell, *Faces at the Bottom of the Well* (New York: Basic Books, 1992); Lois Benjamin, *The Black Elite* (Chicago, Ill.: Nelson-Hall, 1992); Jill Nelson, *Volunteer Slavery* (Chicago, Ill.: Noble Press, 1993); Nathan McCall, *Makes Me Wanna Holler* (New York: Random House, 1994); and Brent Staples, *Parallel Time* (New York: Pantheon, 1994). Sardonic and enlightening observations of the treatment of upper-middle-class blacks in public settings are in Lawrence Otis Graham's *Member of the Club: Reflections on Life in a Racially Polarized World* (New York: HarperCollins, 1995). For a sociological context, see Bart Landry, *The New Black Middle Class* (Berkeley: University of California Press, 1987).

17. "Apartheid on Campus, Continued," *New York Times* (July 4, 1993), p. E10; "Massachusetts Campus Is Torn by Racial Strife," *New York Times* (October 18, 1992), p. 12; "Over 100 Are Arrested in Iowa Campus Brawl," *New York Times* (May 4, 1992), p. A13; "On Once Liberal Campuses, Racial Divide Grows Wider," *New York Times* (October 25, 1995), p. A1. See also John H. Bunzel, *Race Relations on Campus* (Stanford, Calif.: Stanford Alumni Association, 1992).

Chapter 2

1. Sidney Kaplan, *The Black Presence in the Era of the American Revolution: 1770–1800* (Washington, D.C.: Smithsonian Institution Press, 1973), p. 3.

2. Historical studies of blacks in the American armed forces are quite extensive. The standard work is Bernard C. Nalty, *Strength for the Fight: A History of Black Americans in the Military* (New York: Free Press, 1986). See also Bernard C. Nalty and Morris J. MacGregor, *Blacks in the Military: Essential Documents* (Wilmington, Del.: Scholarly Resources, 1981); Morris MacGregor, *Defense Studies: Integration of the Armed Forces* (Washington, D.C.: Center of Military History, 1981); and Ulysses Lee, *The United States Army in World War II, Special Studies: The Employment of Negro Troops* (Wash-

ington, D.C.: Office of the Chief of Military History, 1966). For bibliographies, see Lenwood G. Davis and George Hill, compilers, *Blacks in the American Armed Forces, 1776–1983* (Westport, Conn.: Greenwood Press, 1985); and Department of the Army, *Black Americans in the Military: A Selective Bibliography* (Washington, D.C.: Pentagon Library, 1993). For insightful treatment of broader issues of minorities and military recruitment, see John Whiteclay Chambers II, *To Raise an Army* (New York: Free Press, 1987); David R. Segal, *Recruiting for Uncle Sam* (Lawrence: University Press of Kansas, 1989); and James Burk, "Citizenship Status and Military Service," *Armed Forces and Society*, vol. 21, no. 4 (Summer 1995), pp. 503–30. An excellent legal treatment of the inclusion and exclusion of Americans from full citizenship is Martha Minnow, *Making All the Difference* (Ithaca, N.Y.: Cornell University Press, 1990).

3. Nalty and MacGregor, *Blacks in the Military*, p. 1.

4. Ibid., p. 3.

5. Statutes at Large of South Carolina (vol. 7 [1840], p. 33) in *The Negro in the Military Service of the United States, 1639–1886*, Microfilm M58, National Archives, Washington, D.C.

6. Jack D. Foner, *Blacks and the Military in American History* (New York: Praeger, 1974), pp. 4–5.

7. Kaplan, *Black Presence in the Era of the American Revolution*, p. 1.

8. Nalty and MacGregor, *Blacks in the Military*, p. 7.

9. For a discussion, see Henry M. Minton, "Early History of Negroes in Business in Philadelphia." Paper read before the American Historical Society, March 1913.

10. Benjamin Quarles, *The Negro in the American Revolution* (Chapel Hill: University of North Carolina Press, 1961).

11. USAEUR [U.S. Army Europe] Race Relations School, "Black Soldier, a Compendium," Obtained from the Department of Defense, 1972, p. 1.

12. Nalty and MacGregor, *Blacks in the Military*, p. 7.

13. The total includes both Army and Navy.

14. "Lists and Returns of Connecticut Men in the American Revolutionary War, 1715–1782," Connecticut Historical Society, Collection 12 (1909), pp. 59, 80, 81, 183.

15. USAEUR Race Relations School, "Black Soldier, a Compendium," p. 2.

16. Ibid., p. 5.

17. Richard J. Stillman, *Integration of the Negro in the U.S. Armed Forces* (New York: Frederick Praeger, 1968), p. 9.

18. Nalty and MacGregor, *Blacks in the Military*, p. 19.

19. James M. McPherson, *The Negro's Civil War* (New York: Ballantine Books, 1965), p. 19.

20. Ibid., pp. 19–20.

21. Ibid., p. 20.

22. Ibid., p. 22.

23. For insights into Army life for blacks during the early years of the Civil War, see the diary of the white colonel who commanded the South Carolina Volunteers: Thomas Wentworth Higginson, *Army Life in a Black Regiment* (Boston: Fields, Osgood & Co., 1870).

24. Dwight W. Hoover, *Understanding Negro History* (Chicago, Ill.: Quadrangle Books, 1968), p. 270.

25. John Hope Franklin, *From Slavery to Freedom: A History of Negro Americans* (New York: Alfred A. Knopf, 1964), p. 74.

26. Stillman, *Integration of the Negro in the U.S. Armed Forces*, p. 128.

27. William H. Leckie, *The Buffalo Soldiers* (Norman: University of Oklahoma Press, 1967), p. 6.

28. Herschel Cashin, *Under Fire* (New York: Tennyson Neeley, 1899), p. 147.

29. Stokely Carmichael and Charles Hamilton, *Black Power: The Politics of Liberation in America* (New York: Vintage Books, 1967), p. 26.

30. Nalty and MacGregor, *Blacks in the Military*, p. 76.

31. Ibid., p. 77.

32. David Levering Lewis, *W. E. B. Du Bois: Biography of a Race* (New York: Henry Holt, 1993), p. 555. This important book is vital to anyone seeking to understand the interplay between black consciousness and American identity.

33. John H. Stanfield, "The Dilemma of Conscientious Objection for Afro-Americans," in Charles Moskos and John Whiteclay Chambers II, eds., *The New Conscientious Objection: From Sacred to Secular Resistance* (New York: Oxford University Press, 1993), pp. 47–56.

34. Stephen Ambrose, *The Military and American Society* (New York: Free Press, 1972), p. 196.

35. Ibid., p. 26.

36. August Mier, *Black Protest Thought in the Twentieth Century* (New York: Bobbs-Merrill, 1969), p. 221.

37. Nalty and MacGregor, *Blacks in the Military*, pp. 107–8.

38. The classic sociological work on race in the World War II military remains Samuel A. Stouffer et al., *The American Soldier, Adjustment During Army Life,* vol. 1 (Princeton, N.J.: Princeton University Press, 1949). The section on "Negro Soldiers," pp. 486–599, can still be read today with great edification.

39. The Tuskegee Airmen were the subject of a major Home Box Office movie in 1995. For a comprehensive and recent historical account, see Stanley Sandler, *Segregated Skies: All-Black Combat Squadrons of WW II* (Washington, D.C.: Smithsonian Institution Press, 1992).

40. Benjamin O. Davis, Jr., *American* (Washington, D.C.: Smithsonian Institution Press, 1991).

41. Brenda Moore, *To Serve My Country, To Serve My Race* (New York: New York University Press, 1995).

42. Henry Louis Gates, Jr., *Colored People* (New York: Vintage Books, 1995), pp. 83–84.

43. John P. Davis, *The Negro Reference Book* (Englewood Cliffs, N.J.: Prentice-Hall, 1971), p. 652.

44. Charles C. Moskos, *The American Enlisted Man* (New York: Russell Sage Foundation, 1971), p. 111.

45. On the early days of integration, see Lee Nichols, *Breakthrough on the Color Front* (New York: Random House, 1954); Stillman, *Integration of the Negro in the U.S. Armed Forces*; Richard M. Dalfiume, *Desegregation of the U.S. Armed Forces* (Columbia: University of Missouri Press, 1969); and Leo Bogart, ed., *Social Research and the Desegregation of the U.S. Army* (Chicago, Ill.: Markham, 1969). Especially valuable for the way the services informally as well as officially confronted racial integration is Alan L. Gropman, *The Air Force Integrates: 1945–1964* (Washington, D.C.: Office of Air Force History, 1978).

46. Moskos, *The American Enlisted Man*, p. 111.

47. Ernest Leiser, "For Negroes, It's a New Army Now," *Saturday Evening Post* (December 13, 1952), p. 26.

48. Westat, Inc., *The 1985 Army Experience Survey, Tabular Descriptions of First-Term Separatees*, vol. 1 (Alexandria, Va.: U.S. Army Research Institute for the Behavioral and Social Sciences, 1986), p. 38.

49. Department of Defense, "Information Paper: Montgomery GI Bill and Army College Fund," January 10, 1994.

50. General Accounting Office, *Operation Desert Storm: Race and Gender Comparison of Deployed Forces with All Active Duty Forces*, June 25, 1992.

51. Laura L. Miller and Charles C. Moskos, "Humanitarians or Warriors: Race, Gender and Combat Status in Operation Restore Hope," *Armed Forces and Society*, vol. 21, no. 4 (Summer 1995), pp. 615–38.

Chapter 3

1. Martin Binkin and Mark J. Eitelberg, "Women and Minorities in the All-Volunteer Force," in William Bowman, Roger Little, and G. Thomas Sicilia, eds., *The All-Volunteer Force After a Decade* (Washington, D.C.: Pergamon-Brassey's, 1986), pp. 73–102. See also Martin Binkin, *America's Volunteer Military* (Washington, D.C.: Brookings Institution, 1984).
2. Binkin and Eitelberg, "Women and Minorities in the AVF."
3. "Ranks of Inmates Reach One Million in a 2-Decade Rise," *New York Times* (October 28, 1994), p. A1. Michael Tonry, professor of law at the University of Minnesota, estimates that blacks are seven times more likely than whites to go to prison. *New York Times* (October 5, 1995), p. A8.
4. The movie *Cadence* (1990) captures well the assimilation of a white soldier in the black enlisted culture.
5. National sample from People for the American Way, *Democracy's Next Generation* (Washington, D.C.: People for the American Way, 1992), p. 61. Black NCO sample from 1994 survey conducted by authors; 348 in survey.
6. Charles Fuller, *A Soldier's Play* (New York: Hill & Wang, 1981).
7. Charles A. Hines, "Military Job Performance Evaluation Patterns in Intraracial and Interracial Dyads," unpublished doctoral dissertation, Department of Sociology, Johns Hopkins University, Baltimore, Md., 1983. That this significant work has not been published is a loss to the social scientific community.
8. For example, 39 percent of whites compared with 23 percent of blacks believe "a homosexual can be a good role model for a child." Survey by Yankelovich Partners for *Time* and CNN, June 15–16, 1994.
9. Colin L. Powell with Joseph E. Perisco, *My American Journey* (New York: Random House, 1995), pp. 160–61.

Chapter 4

1. U.S. Army, Information Paper, Judge Advocate General, "Subject: Criminal Prosecutions Under Article 117, Uniform Code of Military Justice, U.S. v. Shropshire (1990)," September 17, 1993.

2. For an insightful account of the early years of the Defense Race Relations Institute and changes in the curriculum as a result of research, see Richard O. Hope, *Racial Strife in the U.S. Military: Toward the Elimination of Discrimination* (New York: Praeger, 1979). See also Peter G. Nordlie and Robert L. Hiett, *Measuring the Impact of Race Relations and Equal Opportunity Programs in the Military* (Washington, D.C.: Human Sciences Research, 1974); and Dan Landis, "Race Relations Training in the American Military," paper presented at the American Psychological Association, Washington, D.C., December 7, 1992.

3. Defense Equal Opportunity Management Institute, "Program of Instruction 1994," pp. 4190–91.

4. Arthur M. Schlesinger, Jr., *The Disuniting of America* (New York: W. W. Norton, 1991). For an insightful critique of multiculturalism, see Amitai Etzioni, "Social Science as a Multicultural Canon," *Society*, vol. 29, no. 1 (November/December 1991), pp. 14–18.

5. Mickey R. Dansby and Dan Landis, "Measuring Equal Opportunity Climate in the Military Environment," *International Journal of Intercultural Relations*, vol. 15, no. 4 (1991), pp. 389–405; Dan Landis, Mickey R. Dansby, and Robert H. Faley, "The Military Equal Opportunity Climate Survey," in Paul Rosenfeld, Jack E. Edwards, and Marie D. Thomas, eds., *Improving Organizational Surveys* (Newbury Park, Calif.: Sage Publications, 1993), pp. 210–37.

6. MEOCS items present various incidents that the respondent characterizes on a scale ranging from "very likely" to "almost no chance that the action occurred." Such incidents include a senior NCO made demeaning comments about minority personnel, graffiti written on the rest room walls "put down" minorities and women, a new minority person joined the unit and quickly developed close white friends from within the unit, majority and minority officers were seen socializing together at off-duty locations, and an officer referred to women subordinates by their first names in public while using ranks for the male subordinates.

7. Army Regulation 600–20, "Command Policy," p. 143.

8. Robert D. Smither and Mary Ruth Houston, "Racial Discrimination and Forms of Redress in the Military," *International Journal of Intercultural Relations*, vol. 15, no. 4 (1991), pp. 459–68.

9. *Uniform Military Justice Code*, Article 117, section 42, paragraph c.

10. U.S. Army, Information Paper, Judge Advocate General, "Subject: Criminal Prosecutions Under Article 117," Uniform Code of Military Justice, September 17, 1993.

11. *R.A.V. v. City of St. Paul, Minnesota*, 112 S Ct. 2538 (1992).

12. On this point, see Henry Louis Gates, Jr., "Let Them Talk," *New Republic* (September 20, 1993), pp. 37–49. Our line of reasoning on differential responses to hate speech relies heavily on Gates's formulation.

13. General Accounting Office, *Military Equal Opportunity: Certain Trends in Racial and Gender Data*, NSIAD–95–169 (Washington, D.C.: Government Printing Office, 1995).

14. For a good analysis of the issues in the legal case in which white officers state that the application of affirmative action to Army promotions is unconstitutional, see Katherine McIntire, "Hitting the Boards," *Army Times*, 4 (May 1992), pp. 14–15.

15. Deborah J. Carter and Reginald Wilson, *Minorities in Higher Education 1994* (Washington, D.C.: American Council on Higher Education, 1995), p. 284.

16. On how the shortage of qualified blacks distorts affirmative action, see Michael S. Greve, "The Newest Move in Law Schools' Quota Games," *Wall Street Journal* (October 5, 1992), p. 12A.

17. *Journal of Blacks in Higher Education*, no. 5 (Autumn 1994), p. 44.

18. Seymour Martin Lipset, *Equality and the American Creed: Understanding the Affirmative Action Debate* (Washington, D.C.: Progressive Policy Institute, June 1991). Also germane is Will Marshall, *From Preferences to Empowerment: A New Bargain on Affirmative Action* (Washington, D.C.: Progressive Policy Institute, August 1995).

19. An excellent compilation of much of this research is found in James A. Thomas, ed., *Race Relations Research in the U.S. Army in the 1970s* (Alexandria, Va.: Army Research Institute for the Behavioral and Social Sciences, 1988).

20. John Sibley Butler, "Inequality in the Military: An Examination of Promotion Time for Black and White Enlisted Personnel," *American Sociological Review*, vol. 41 (October 1976), pp. 558–66.

Chapter 5

1. Good discussion of the relevant literature dealing with test scores is found in Bernard R. Gifford and Linda C. Wing, eds.,

Test Policy in Defense (Boston, Mass.: Kluwer Academic Publishers, 1992).

2. John V. McCarthy, president of Control Data Corporation, donated $300,000 in CYBIS value.

3. Jane S. Borne, *A Plan to Implement a Pre-Military Development Program* (Gulfport: University of Mississippi, June 1991).

4. For excellent summaries of the literature and research on underqualified entrants into the military, see Janice H. Laurence and Peter F. Ramsberger, *Low-Aptitude Men in the Military* (New York: Praeger, 1991); and Thomas G. Sticht et al., *Cast-Off Youth* (New York: Praeger, 1987).

5. Ibid.

6. Similar prep schools exist for the Air Force and the Navy. The Army Prep School places more emphasis on recruiting enlisted members into the school than the prep schools of the sister services. For an unsympathetic evaluation of the military prep schools, see American Council on Education, *Service Academy Preparatory Schools Report* (Washington, D.C.: American Council on Education, May 6, 1993).

7. General Accounting Office, *DOD Service Academies* (Washington, D.C.: Government Printing Office, March 1992).

8. Christopher Jencks, *Rethinking Social Policy* (Cambridge, Mass.: Harvard University Press, 1992), p. 19.

Chapter 6

1. The term was coined by John Sibley Butler in *Entrepreneurship and Self-Help Among Black Americans: A Reconsideration of Race and Economics* (New York: State University of New York Press, 1991).

2. Charles Johnson, *The Negro College Graduate* (Chapel Hill: University of North Carolina Press, 1938), pp. 80–81.

5. C. Van Woodward, *Origins of the New South* (Baton Rouge: Louisiana State University Press, 1971).

6. For an extended discussion and listing of these schools, see Butler, *Entrepreneurship and Self-Help*, pp. 80–96.

7. "Black Boarding Schools Filling a Growing Need," *New York Times* (September 21, 1994), pp. 1, B12.

8. Henry Louis Gates, Jr., recounts his boyhood in a segregated environment where academic excellence was not only encouraged but also expected by the middle class that set the standard for all blacks. Henry Louis Gates, Jr., *Colored People: A Memoir* (New York: Vintage, 1995).

9. Andrew Billingsley, *Climbing Jacob's Ladder: The Enduring Legacy of African-American Families* (New York: Simon & Schuster, 1992). This is a classic sociological understanding of the black family in America. See also the prominent interweaving of military service and Afro-American history in Benjamin Quarles, *The Negro in the Making of America* (New York: Collier Books, 1987).

10. A conceptual approach to the responsibilities of the black middle class to transmit self-help values to working-class and poor Afro-Americans is Roy L. Brooks, *Rethinking the American Race Problem* (Berkeley: University of California Press, 1990).

11. On a ratio of one equals parity with the national population, black southerners comprise 1.7 of the Army's career forces, black northerners 1.3, white southerners 1.2, and white northerners 0.9.

12. Since that conversation, Shirley Bender has become a vice president at the University of Texas at Arlington.

13. For the positive effects of military service on black veterans' earnings, see Harley L. Browning, Sally C. Lopreato, and Dudley L. Poston, Jr., "Income and Veteran Status," *American Sociological Review*, vol. 38 (February 1973), pp. 74–85; Sally C. Lopreato and Dudley L. Poston, Jr., "Differences in Earnings and Earnings Ability Between Black Veterans and Nonveterans in the United States," *Social Science Quarterly*, vol. 57 (March 1977), pp. 750–66; Dudley L. Poston, Jr., "Military Service and the Civilian Earnings Patterns of Black and Mexican American Men," Final Report of Research Grant No. SOC–76–10665 to the National Science Foundation, 1979; Melanie Martindale and Dudley L. Poston, Jr., "Variations in Veteran-Nonveteran Earnings Patterns Among World War II, Korea, and Vietnam War Cohorts," *Armed Forces and Society*, vol. 5 (Winter 1979), pp. 219–43; Roger D. Little and J. Eric Fredland, "Veteran Status, Earnings, and Race," *Armed Forces and Society*, vol. 5 (Winter 1979), pp. 244–60; Dudley L. Poston, Jr., "The Effects of Military Service on the Civilian Earnings of White Veterans and Nonveterans," Final Report of Research Grant No. SOC–78–05283 to the National Science Foundation, 1981; and Curtis L. Gilroy et al., "The Economic Returns to Military Service: Race-Ethnic Differences," Research Report 91–1, Office of the Assistant Secretary of Defense (Force Management and Personnel), August 1991.

For more negative accounts, see Phillips Cutright, "The Civilian Earnings of White and Black Draftees and Nonveterans," *American Sociological Review*, vol. 39, no. 3 (1974), pp. 317–27; Joshua D. Angrist, "The Effect of Veterans Benefits on Education and Earnings," *Industrial and Labor Relations Review*, vol. 46, no. 4 (July 1993), pp. 637–52; and Joshua D. Angrist, "Using the Draft Lottery to Measure the Effects of Military Service on Civilian Labor Market Outcomes," in Ron Ehrenberg, ed., *Research in Labor Economics* 10 (Greenwich, Conn.: JAI Press, 1989).

For a good summary of the state of the research findings, see Jere Cohen, David R. Segal, and Lloyd V. Temme, "The Impact of Education on Vietnam-Era Veterans' Occupational Attainment," *Social Science Quarterly*, vol. 73, no. 2 (June 1992), pp. 397–409; and Jere Cohen, Rebbeca L. Warner, and David R. Segal, "Military Service and Educational Attainment in the All-Volunteer Force," *Social Science Quarterly*, vol. 76, no. 1 (March 1995), pp. 88–104.

For an explicit discussion of the military as an avenue of upward mobility, see Robert D. Mare and Christopher Winship, "The Paradox of Lessening Racial Inequality and Joblessness Among Black Youth: Enrollment, Enlistment, and Employment 1964–81," *American Sociological Review*, vol. 49, no. 1 (January 1984), pp. 39–55.

14. John Modell, Marc Goulden, and Sigurdur Magnusson, "World War II in the Lives of Black Americans," *Journal of American History*, vol. 76, no. 3 (December 1989), pp. 838–48.

15. Ibid., p. 848.

16. Browning, Lopreato, and Poston, "Income and Veteran Status." See also Yu Xie, "The Socioeconomic Status of Young Male Veterans, 1964–1984," *Social Science Quarterly*, vol. 73, no. 2 (June 1992), pp. 379–91.

17. Paul A. Gade, Hyder Lakhani, and Melvin Kimmel, "Military Service: A Good Place to Start," *Military Psychology*, vol. 3, no. 4 (1991), pp. 251–67. See also Paul A. Gade, "The U.S. Army: Black Veterans Review Their Experience," Personnel Utilization Technical Area Working Paper, U.S. Army Research Institute for the Behavioral and Social Sciences, June 1986.

18. Christopher G. Ellison, "Military Background, Racial Orientation, and Political Participation Among Black Adult Males,"

Social Science Quarterly, vol. 73, no. 2 (June 1992), pp. 360–78.

19. George H. Lawrence and Thomas D. Kane, "Military Service and Racial Attitudes of White Veterans," *Armed Forces and Society*, vol. 22, no. 2 (Winter 1996). Also relevant is M. Kent Jennings and Gregory B. Markus, "The Effects of Military Service on Political Attitudes: A Panel Study," *American Political Science Review*, vol. 71, no. 1 (March 1977), pp. 131–47.

20. A revealing analysis of ways whites and blacks differ in their interpretation of events is Lawrence Bobo et al., "Public Opinion Before and After a Spring of Discontent," in Mark Bladassare, ed., *The Los Angeles Riots* (Boulder, Colo.: Westview, 1994), pp. 103–34. An especially good summary of attitudinal differences between blacks and whites, because it looks at survey differences within the races, is Jennifer L. Hocschild, *Facing Up to the American Dream: Race, Class, and the Soul of the Nation* (Princeton, N.J.: Princeton University Press, 1995).

21. Milton D. Morris, "African Americans and the New World Order," *Washington Quarterly*, vol. 15, no. 2 (Autumn 1992), pp. 5–21; Dianne M. Pinderhughes, "The Case of African Americans in the Persian Gulf," in Janet Dwart, ed., *The State of Black America 1991* (New York: National Urban League, 1991); Arch Puddington, "Black Leaders vs. Desert Storm," *Commentary* (May 1991), pp. 28–34.

22. 1992 survey conducted for Joint Center for Political and Economic Studies, Washington, D.C. Courtesy of Milton D. Morris.

23. A. Wade Smith, "Attitudes Toward the Racial Composition of the Military," in Edwin Dorn, ed., *Who Defends America? Race, Sex and Class in the Armed Forces* (Washington, D.C.: Joint Center for Political and Economic Studies, 1989), p. 117. See also A. Wade Smith, "Public Consciousness of Blacks in the Military," *Journal of Political and Military Sociology*, vol. 11, no. 2, p. 117; and John Sibley Butler and Margaret A. Johnson, "An Overview of the Relationships Between Demographic Characteristics of Americans and Their Attitudes Towards Military Issues," *Journal of Political and Military Sociology*, vol. 19, no. 2 (Winter 1991), pp. 272–92.

24. CBS News Poll, *New York Times* (December 14, 1990), p. A8.

25. *Wall Street Journal*/NBC News Poll, "Low Expectations" (September 30, 1994), pp. A1, 5.

26. Vernon E. Jordan, Jr., "Look Outward Black America," *Wall Street Journal* (October 27, 1995), p. A14. Jordan lists five

areas with new black leaders: elected officials, managers of public institutions, community leaders, entrepreneurs, and corporate America.

27. *Jet* (February 25, 1991), p. 34.

28. Cornell West, *Race Matters* (Boston, Mass.: Beacon Press, 1993), p. 54.

29. Survey data consistently show blacks being less receptive to gay rights than whites. See, for example, reference cited in note 8 for chapter 3, above.

30. Juan Williams, "President Colin Powell?" *Reconstruction*, vol. 2, no. 3 (1994), p. 78.

31. In addition to Colin Powell's autobiography, *My American Journey* (New York: Random House, 1995), the reader is also directed to two earlier biographies: Howard Means, *Colin Powell* (New York: Ballantine Books, 1992); and David Roth, *Sacred Honor* (Grand Rapids, Mich.: Zondervan, 1993). Another insightful interview (besides Williams's "President Colin Powell?") is Henry Louis Gates, Jr., "Powell and the Black Elite," *New Yorker* (September 25, 1995), pp. 64–80.

32. Remarks of Colin L. Powell for the annual convention of the National Association for the Advancement of Colored People, Houston, Texas, July 11, 1991.

33. Junior Reserve Officers' Training Corps (JROTC) costs $900 per student; the federal government contributes only one-third of this and the rest is paid by the local school system. Students in JROTC are organized into small units as in the military to develop teamwork and leadership skills. They study the U.S. Constitution and the Bill of Rights and discuss the rights and responsibilities of living in a democracy. Critics of JROTC regard it as a form of militarization and have prevented JROTC from entering the public school systems in several cities. Gay-rights activists have also contested JROTC units because of the military's de facto ban on homosexuals.

34. Students in JROTC are not taught military skills per se, but do participate in color guard and drill activities. The instructors are retired military officers or noncommissioned officers. Once a week, the cadets wear military-style uniforms to school. Critics of JROTC regard it as form of military recruitment. In fact, about half of the Army's JROTC's 11,000 students who graduated in 1993 did go on to serve in the military or to enter college ROTC programs.

35. Powell, *My American Journey*, pp. 555–56.

36. Williams, "President Colin Powell?" p. 76.

37. Colin L. Powell, Commencement Address, Fisk University, Nashville, Tenn., May 4, 1992.

38. Williams, "President Colin Powell?" p. 72.

39. Gates, "Powell and the Black Elite," p. 66.

40. *Essence* (November 1992), p. 125.

41. Colin Powell, Commencement Address, Howard University, Washington, D.C., May 14, 1994.

42. In 1995 a black major accused the Air Force Academy of removing him from a teaching position because he acts "too black." Major Gregory Russell said he was demoted because he wears earrings, baggy pants, and backward baseball caps —while off-duty but on base. Colorado Springs *Gazette Telegraph* (June 22, 1995), p. B2. Why such garb should be considered "black" is left unclear.

43. Colin L. Powell, Convocation Speech, Lawson State College, Birmingham, Ala., March 12, 1993.

Chapter 7

1. Also, as Mickey Kaus points out in *The End of Equality* (New York: Basic Books, 1992), variations in pay and fringe benefits will become more pronounced. The American economy is increasingly subject to a "Hollywood effect," in which outstanding performers are paid far better than those a notch below in talent.

2. Federal Glass Ceiling Commission, *Good for Business: Making Full Use of the Nation's Human Capital* (Washington, D.C.: Government Printing Office, 1995), p. 9.

3. Lawrence Otis Graham, *The Best Companies for Minorities: Employers Across America Who Recruit, Train, and Promote Minorities* (New York: Penguin, 1993).

4. Richard L. Zweigenhaft and G. William Domhoff, *Blacks in the White Establishment?* (New Haven, Conn.: Yale University Press, 1991).

5. Ibid., p. 162.

6. Anthony S. Byrk, Valerie E. Lewe, and Peter B. Holland, *Catholic Schools and the Common Good* (Cambridge, Mass.: Harvard University Press, 1993).

7. James Fallows, "Military Efficiency," *Atlantic Monthly* (August 1991), p. 18.

8. Harley L. Browning, Sally C. Lopreato, and Dudley L. Poston, Jr., "Income and Veteran Status," *American Sociological Review*, vol. 38 (February 1973), pp. 74–85.

9. For the definitive discussion on how non–means-tested programs lead to powerful political constituencies, see Theda Skocpol, *Social Policy in the United States* (Princeton, N.J.: Princeton University Press, 1995). See also Skocpol, "Investing in Young Americans: Lessons from the GI Bill of 1944," Franklin and Eleanor Roosevelt Institute, Harvard University, 1996, unpublished paper.

10. Peter Kolchin, *American Slavery, 1619–1877* (New York: Hill & Wang, 1993). See also Sterling Stuckey, *Slave Culture: Nationalist Theory and the Foundations of Black America* (New York: Oxford University Press, 1987); and Clovis E. Semmes, *Cultural Hegemony and African American Development* (Westport, Conn.: Praeger, 1992).

11. Eric J. Sundquist, *To Wake the Nations: Race in the Making of American Literature* (Cambridge, Mass.: Harvard University Press, 1994).

12. Shelly Fisher Fishkin, *Was Huck Black? Mark Twain and African-American Voices* (New York: Oxford University Press, 1994).

13. Harold Bloom, "African-American Religions as Paradigm," in his *The American Religion* (New York: Simon & Schuster, 1992), pp. 237–55. See also Hans A. Baer and Merrill Singer, *African-American Religion in the Twentieth Century* (Knoxville: University of Tennessee Press, 1994).

14. Joseph M. Murphy, *Working the Spirit: Ceremonies of the African Diaspora* (Boston, Mass.: Beacon Press, 1993).

15. Harvey Cox, *Fire from Heaven: The Rise of Pentecostal Spirituality and the Reshaping of Religion in the Twenty-first Century* (Reading, Mass.: Addison-Wesley, 1994).

16. Stephen Carter, *Culture of Disbelief* (New York: Basic Books, 1993).

17. Celeste Michelle Condit and John Louis Lucaites, *Crafting Equality: America's Anglo-African Word* (Chicago, Ill.: University of Chicago Press, 1993). See also Sterling Stuckey, *Going Through the Storm: The Influence of African American Art in History* (New York: Oxford University Press, 1994).

18. Henry Louis Gates, Jr., "A Fragmented Man: George Schuyler and the Claims of Race," *New York Times Book Review* (September 20, 1992), pp. 31, 42–43.

19. Mel Watkins, *On the Real Side* (New York: Simon & Schuster, 1994).

20. In Ralph Ellison, "What America Would Be Like Without Blacks," cited in *Atlantic Monthly* (March 1995), p. 67.

21. Cornell West, *Race Matters* (Boston, Mass.: Beacon Press, 1993), p. 2.

22. Nathan Irvin Huggins, *Revelations: American History, American Myth* (New York: Oxford University Press, 1995), p. 127.

23. Ishmael Reed, *Airing Dirty Laundry* (Reading, Mass.: Addison-Wesley, 1993), p. 273.

24. Lerone Bennett, Jr., *Before the Mayflower: A History of Black America* (New York: Penguin, 1993).

25. For a fuller explication of the view, see Peter C. Moskos, "Afro-Anglo: America's Core Culture," *National Journal of Sociology*, 1996, in press.

26. Michael Berube, "Public Academy," *New Yorker* (January 9, 1995), pp. 73–80. See also the cover story by Robert S. Boynton, "The New Intellectuals," *Atlantic Monthly* (March 1995), pp. 53–70.

27. A partial listing of such public intellectuals includes K. Anthony Appiah, Derrick Bell, Tony Brown, Bebe Moore Campbell, Stephen L. Carter, Ellis Cose, Stanley Crouch, Michael Eric Dyson, Gerald Early, Henry Louis Gates, Jr., Nikki Giovani, Lani Guinier, Steven A. Holmes, bell hooks, Nathan Irvin Huggins, Randall Kennedy, Alan Keyes, C. Eric Lincoln, Glenn C. Loury, Clarence Page, Orlando Patterson, Alphonse Pinckney, William Raspberry, Adolph L. Reed, Jr., Ishmael Reed, Carl T. Rowan, Thomas Sowell, Brent Staples, Shelby Steele, Ronald Walters, Cornel West, Ralph Wiley, Roger Wilkins, Juan Williams, Patricia Williams, Walter Williams, William Julius Wilson, as well as many others.

28. John Hope Franklin, "The New Negro History," in *Race and History* (Baton Rouge: Louisiana State University, 1989), p. 47.

29. Shelby Steele, "Affirmative Action Must Go," *New York Times* (March 1, 1995), p. A13.

30. Gordon W. Allport, *The Nature of Prejudice* (Garden City, N.Y.: 1958), p. 263.

31. Robert J. Sampson and John H. Laub, "Socioeconomic Achievement in the Life Course of Disadvantaged Men: Military Service as a Turning Point, Circa 1940–1965," *American Sociological Review*, vol. 61, no. 3 (June 1996), pp. 347–67.

32. For a thoughtful piece on the effects on Afro-American achievement of a thin representation of blacks at elite schools, see Steve Sailer, "Where the Races Relate," *National Review* (November 27, 1995), pp. 41–44.

33. See the story on the Office of Federal Contract Compliance Programs by Steven A. Holmes, "Once-Tough Chief of Affir-

mative-Action Agency Is Forced to Change Tack," *New York Times* (August 6, 1995), p. A13.

34. *Navy Times* (May 1, 1995), p. 14.

35. Starting in 1995, Navy recruiters have been authorized to make an Immediate Selection Decision (ISD) to offer a minority student a Navy ROTC scholarship. In the first year, not a single black had been placed in the program because eligibility requires a minimum SAT score of 600 in mathematics.

36. In 1995, the number of Reserve Officer Training Corps (ROTC) units at historically black colleges by service was Army 27, Air Force 6, and Navy 5.

37. On the noncomparability of black Americans and other ethnic groups, we follow Stanley Lieberson, *A Piece of the Pie: Black and White Immigrants Since 1880* (Berkeley: University of California Press, 1980); and Nathan Irving Huggins, "Ethnic Americans," in his *Revelations: American History, American Myths* (New York: Oxford University Press, 1995), pp. 148–57. For a summary of studies on how whites treat blacks differently, see Thomas F. Pettigrew and Joanne Martin, "Shaping the Organizational Context for Black American Inclusion," *Journal of Social Issues*, vol. 43, no. 1 (1987), pp. 41–78. See also Orlando Patterson and Chris Winship, "White Poor, Black Poor," *New York Times* (May 3, 1992), p. 17; and Orlando Patterson, "Affirmative Action on the Merit System," *New York Times* (August 7, 1995), p. A11.

38. One of the most sophisticated arguments for class-based affirmative action is Richard Kahlenberg, "Class, Not Race," *New Republic* (April 3, 1995), pp. 21–27; and Kahlenberg, "Equal Opportunity Critics," *New Republic* (July 17, 24, 1995), pp. 20–25. For a formulation of affirmative action that comes closer to our position, see Jeffrey Rosen, "Affirmative Action: A Solution," *New Republic* (May 8, 1995), pp. 20–25; and Will Marshall, *From Preferences to Empowerment: A New Bargain on Affirmative Action* (Washington, D.C.: Progressive Policy Institute, August 1995).

39. John Sibley Butler, "Multiple Identities," *Society* (May/June 1990), pp. 8–13. Michael Lind goes further, arguing that black Americans are more American than most white Americans. See his *The Next American Nation* (New York: Free Press, 1995), pp. 274–76.

40. Benjamin O. Davis, Jr., *American* (Washington, D.C.: Smithsonian Institution Press, 1991); Colin L. Powell, *My American Journey* (New York: Random House, 1995).

Appendix

1. On implications of the military drawdown, see David W. Grissmer, *Impact of the Military Drawdown on Youth Employment, Training and Educational Opportunity* (Santa Monica, Calif.: RAND, 1992); Kara B. Richards and Gary L. Bowen, "Military Downsizings and Its Potential Implications for Hispanic, Black, and White Soldiers," *Journal of Primary Prevention*, vol. 14, no. 1 (1993), pp. 73–92; and Rhonda J. Moore, "The Historical and Cultural Effects of Post–Cold War Downsizing on Racial and Gender Inclusion in the United States Marine Corps," Ph.D. dissertation, Department of Anthropology, Stanford University, Stanford, Calif., forthcoming.

2. William James, "The Moral Equivalent of War," in *Essays on Faith and Morals* ([1910], New York: Longman, Greens, 1943), pp. 311–28.

3. For a discussion of James's pacifism, see Gerald E. Meyers, *William James* (New Haven, Conn.: Yale University Press, 1986), pp. 435–45.

4. Robert Coles, *The Call of Service* (Boston, Mass.: Houghton Mifflin, 1993).

5. Morris Janowitz, *The Reconstruction of Patriotism* (Chicago, Ill.: University of Chicago Press, 1983).

6. For a fuller treatment of the history of national service, see Charles Moskos, *A Call to Civic Service* (New York: Free Press, 1988). See also Donald J. Eberly, *National Service: A Promise to Keep* (Rochester, N.Y.: John Alden Books, 1988). An incisive examination of the genesis and development of the AmeriCorps program is Steven Waldman, *The Bill: How the Adventures of Clinton's National Service Bill Reveal What Is Corrupt, Comic, Cynical—and Noble—About Washington* (New York: Viking, 1995).

7. U.S. Advisory Commission on Universal Training, *Program for National Security* (Washington, D.C.: Government Printing Office, 1947), p. 391.

8. National Association of Service and Conservation Members, *Youth Corps Profiles 1993* (Washington, D.C.: NASCC, 1993). All told, the NASCC identified 104 state and local programs, but the demographic data are based on the 89 programs that responded to the survey.

9. An especially insightful book on race relations and other social realities in the Boston program is Suzanne Goldsmith, *A City Year* (New York: New Press, 1993).

10. Democratic Leadership Council, *Citizenship and National Service* (Washington, D.C.: Democratic Leadership Council, 1988).

11. "Foundation Expenses Questioned," *Chicago Tribune* (January 10, 1995), p. 6.

12. Report of the Commission on National and Community Service, *What You Can Do for Your Country* (Washington, D.C.: Commission on National and Community Service, January 1993).

13. Steven Waldman, *The Bill: How the Adventures of Clinton's National Service Bill Reveal What Is Corrupt, Comic, Cynical—and Noble—About Washington*, p. 23.

14. "A First Step Toward AmeriCorps," *USA Today* (September 12, 1994), p. 9.

15. Steven Waldman, "Ask Not—'90s Style," *Newsweek* (September 20, 1993), p. 46.

16. Juri Toomepuu, *Effects of a National Service Program on Army Recruiting* (Fort Sheridan, Ill.: U.S. Army Recruiting Command, 1989).

17. *Chicago Tribune* (March 14, 1995), p. 15.

18. George H. Gallup International Institute, *Attitudes Toward AmeriCorps* (Princeton, N.J.: Gallup International Institute, September 1995), pp. 5, 9.

19. William F. Buckley, Jr., *Gratitude* (New York: Random House, 1990).

20. James J. Pinkerton, *What Comes Next* (New York: Hyperion, 1995), pp. 312–16.

21. A General Accounting Office study estimated that each AmeriCorps participant costs the federal government $17,600 per year. In addition, another $8,000 per enrollee came from local government and private funding sources. General Accounting Office, *National Service Programs* (Washington, D.C.: General Accounting Office, August 1995). The per capita federal costs for a Peace Corps volunteer in 1995 was $33,000. The most careful analysis of AmeriCorps programs concluded that the measurable benefits to the community ranged between $1.60 and $2.60 for each $1.00 in federal outlays. On this, see George R. Neuman et al., *The Benefits and Costs of National Service* (Washington, D.C.: Kormendi/Gardner Partners, 1995).

22. Gallup, *Attitudes Toward AmeriCorps*, p. 93.

23. Ibid., p. 115.

24. "Troops for Teachers," officially the Teachers and Teacher's Aide Placement Assistance Program, is a Pentagon-operated

effort to help veterans find jobs in the classroom. The program was devised by Senators Sam Nunn (D-Ga.), John C. Danforth (R-Mo.), and Edward M. Kennedy (D-Mass.) to help mustered-out service members survive the military drawdown. The bill was also viewed as a practical way to bring badly needed role models into the inner city. DANTES (Defense Activity for Non-Traditional Education Support) was set up in 1992 to help noncommissioned officers gain teacher certification. In 1994, the program was funded at $65 million a year; it offers military persons up to $5,000 each to gain teacher certification. In addition, schools with high enrollments of poor youths receive an inducement—$50,000 in subsidies for the first five years of the former military members' salaries if they hire them as teachers.

Troops for Teachers has been one of the most successful programs of a broader effort to help former service members into second careers. By 1995, some 5,300 former service members had applied for the program, and 167 had been placed in teaching jobs across the country. Early accounts have been favorable, although skeptics state that the ex-service members are hired more because of the salary subsidy than because they are the best suited for the job. Afro-Americans comprise about a quarter of the Troops for Teachers, and most of them teach in inner-city schools.

25. In 1993 Congress directed the Secretary of Defense to start a pilot community outreach to combat drug abuse among young people. The premise was that the military milieu has special strengths—ethnic diversity, a predominantly male makeup—that produce military personnel with special skills, including mentoring skills, that would be effective in drug prevention programs. These people would be especially effective in activities that stressed outdoor adventure, physical fitness, and discipline through activities such as uniformed drill teams. In the first year, the pilot program enrolled about 10,000 youths. Operating the program cost the Defense Department $100 to $600 per enrollee beyond the normal costs for military personnel. An initial evaluation yielded positive findings, especially for programs run by National Guard volunteers.

26. For a prospectus on the use of the National Guard for high school dropouts, see Center for Strategic and International Studies, "Forging a Military Youth Corps" (Washington, D.C.: CSIS, 1992).

27. *New York Times*, "Week in Review" (December 25, 1994), p. 13.

28. Good analyses of the problems and potential of national service in light of the AmeriCorps experience are found in Fran Rothstein, ed., *Perspectives on the Federal Role in National and Community Service* (Washington, D.C.: Youth Service America, 1995). The contributors, however, consistently shy away from any military analogies.

29. Juergen Kuhlmann and Ekkehard Lippert, "The Federal Republic of Germany: Conscientious Objection as Social Welfare," in Charles C. Moskos and John Whiteclay Chambers II, eds., *The New Conscientious Objection* (New York: Oxford University Press, 1993), pp. 98–105.

30. Amitai Etzioni, *A Responsive Society* (San Francisco: Jossey-Bass Publishers, 1991).

Index